DEVELOPING YOUR SECRET
CLOSET OF PRAYER

Endorsements

The author's transparency with personal illustrations along with fundamental precepts on how to develop a private prayer life, including Scripture praying, have been most inspiring, practical and life-changing!

—T. W. in Washington

The principles outlined in *Developing Your Secret Closet of Prayer* have revolutionized the quality of my personal prayer life. The first time I read it, I knew I had discovered a very new and dynamic pathway to reach the heart of God.

—A. I. in Greece

This book, *Developing Your Secret Closet of Prayer,* has drastically changed my prayer life. Prior to reading this book, my prayer time was practically nonexistent, except for spontaneous prayer. This work has truly changed my relationship with God.

—M. P. in New York

By reading *Developing Your Secret Closet of Prayer,* I have received a fresh awareness of an infinite God who willingly invites finite man to come into His presence and commune with Him. What an awesome truth! Oh, what I have been missing!

—B. G. in Hawaii

This book has been a breath of fresh air! It has clarified the simplicity of Scripture praying and the need for the "early morning briefing session" and has reinforced the truth that this is where the battle of the Christian life is won or lost.

—B. F. in Florida

Foreword by BILL BRIGHT

DEVELOPING YOUR SECRET CLOSET *of* PRAYER

with STUDY GUIDE

BECAUSE SOME SECRETS ARE HEARD ONLY IN SOLITUDE

RICHARD A. BURR

with ARNOLD R. FLEAGLE

WingSpread Publishers
Camp Hill, Pennsylvania

WingSpread Publishers
3825 Hartzdale Drive · Camp Hill, PA 17011
www.wingspreadpublishers.com

A division of Zur Ltd.

Developing Your Secret Closet of Prayer, Revised Edition
ISBN: 978-1-60066-180-8
LOC Control Number: 2007941143
© 1998 by Zur Ltd.
Study Guide © 2005 by Richard A. Burr

Previously published by Christian Publications, Inc.
First Christian Publications Edition 1998
First WingSpread Publishers Edition 2008

Cover Design by Design Source Creative Services, Inc.

To my precious princess, Anastasia,
who is truly the physical manifestation
of God's grace in my life.
Thank you, dearest,
for being my best friend
and faithful co-laborer
over these wonderful years!

Contents

In Solitude with God
by
Anastasia I. Burr

To the solitude of prayer
God invites His child alone;
He delights when you, with meekness
And by faith, approach His throne.

In the solitude of prayer,
That communion of love;
God reveals His glorious secrets
Planned for you in heaven above.

To the solitude of prayer
You must go yourself to hide;
Then in peace and joy and gladness
Will your heart for sure abide.

In the solitude of prayer
Pray the Scriptures to the Lord;
So you'll always be victorious
Through His own two-edged sword.

Through the Scriptures in your praying
And His Spirit in your heart,
He will always show His pathways
And His mighty strength impart.

'Tis in quietness and prayer
You will hear His gentle voice;
Thus when flesh and Satan whisper
You shall make the godly choice.

In the solitude of prayer
On your soul He sheds His light;
Then you walk with deep assurance
In the day and in the night.

Go in solitude for prayer,
Daily meet the Lord most high;
When you frequent this His dwelling
You shall know He's always nigh.

Foreword

There is no greater privilege than to be able to communicate directly with our glorious and majestic heavenly Father, the Creator of the entire universe of more than 100 billion galaxies, of which our own galaxy is only a pinprick of light.

This wonderful privilege, of course, is provided only through the blood atonement of God's only begotten Son, our Lord and Savior Jesus Christ, who "died for our sins . . . was buried . . . [and] was raised on the third day according to the Scriptures" (1 Corinthians 15:3-4).

Because of what our Lord Jesus did on our behalf, due to His great love, and the way provided by Him into the heavenly Holy of Holies, we can, by faith, come boldly before God's actual throne and presence, according to Hebrews 4:16. We can actually *communicate* with God Almighty; and He desires—even commands—that we do so! We do it in our "secret closet of prayer."

In *Developing Your Secret Closet of Prayer*, my dear friend Dick Burr provides helpful scriptural insights for us as we exercise this precious privilege. His insights do not involve rigid or ritualistic rules but spiritual principles that will help us remove any hindrances to prayer and lead us to pray in the manner our Lord instructed us when on the earth.

I pray that the principles of this book will help bring each reader into a more intimate, moment-by-moment dialogue and relationship with our wonderful Lord.

Dr. Bill Bright (1921-2003)
Founder and past president,
Campus Crusade for Christ International

Preface

The footprints of my Christian pilgrimage reveal that a significant amount of my journey has been invested in the study of the principles and practice of prayer. A graduate-level course at Grace Seminary increased my appetite. A doctoral dissertation at Gordon Conwell Theological Seminary enlarged my exposure to this discipline through linguistic studies, continental and American scholars and 340 Scripture passages.

Still, I was in for an enlightening surprise at a district ministers' and wives' retreat in northeastern Ohio in the winter of 1996. A guest speaker, Richard Burr, led seminars on "Developing Your Secret Closet of Prayer." Despite all my prior study and writing, I discovered that his words were escorting me through virgin territory and allowing me to taste new biblical and practical truths on communicating with my heavenly Father and His Son, Jesus Christ. Richard's instruction and invitation to practice Scripture praying led me to a new model for my daily devotions.

I approached Richard and asked if he had ever written a book on this seminar. He admitted that he had not, although a mission statement of his ministry included such a goal. He agreed to pursue the idea further, and I am pleased that he has been gracious to include me in a supporting role.

Our task has been made feasible by Priscella Lewis, a member of Stow Alliance Fellowship in Stow, Ohio, who diligently, and at times relentlessly, translated Richard's seminar tapes into a working manuscript.

I was taught to ask this question after I preach: "Did this Sunday's sermon make any difference to the congregation that heard it?" I believe a similar question could be asked of a book: "Does this book make any difference to its readers?" I am confident that as you read *Developing Your Secret Closet of Prayer* your answer will be a resounding "Yes!" The contents of this book have changed my private prayer life and strategically changed the devotional life of many in the congregation I now serve.

By His grace,
Arnold R. Fleagle

Acknowledgments

The author is indeed grateful for an unexpected phone call from Dr. Fleagle following a pastors'/wives' retreat in February 1996. From that conversation evolved the challenge to write this book. Even though I had previously been encouraged to write on this subject, I lacked the confidence to embark on such a project. However, through Arnie's constant encouragement and continued assurance that he would work with me in polishing the manuscript—and after much prayer—we sensed that it was God's will for us to begin the writing process. For this I thank the Lord and will be eternally indebted to my good friend and co-laborer, Dr. Arnold Fleagle.

Also, I want to express my appreciation to my gifted editor, David Fessenden, who took this manuscript and massaged it into its final format. Thank you, my dear friend!

I would be remiss if I did not express my deepest appreciation to my elders—the board of directors of Pray • Think • Act Ministries, Inc. (PTAM)—for their dedication, generosity and wisdom in superintending the affairs of this ministry. These men—Kenneth A. Nelson, Macdonald West, Stephen M. Westbrook and Pastor Donald D. Schaeffer—are extraordinary men of God who have kept me accountable to the call of God in my personal life as well as in my public ministry. And I am grateful to David C. Kennaday, our corporate treasurer, who has given unselfishly of his time and talent to be certain that all financial aspects of this ministry meet the highest standards of integrity and excellence.

I am constrained to mention five former board members whom God used to not only raise up this ministry from its embryonic stages but also to formulate its duty, doctrine and direction. First is Richard D. Mayer (1923-1999), who funded our family's first-year salary when I left the corporate world to enter full-time vocational ministry in 1975.

Second is the late J. Edwin Orr (1912-1987), who was my mentor, associate and advocate. It was he who taught me the doctrine of prayer and its role in reviving the soul and the Church and in awakening the masses. His overwhelming influence has been foundational to all my teaching and is woven throughout the chapters of this book. It was Dr. Orr who insisted that PTAM be a faith ministry and taught me to live by faith.

Next is my dear friend Ralph C. Osborn, who worked with me in laying out the corporate structure, ministry plans and budgets and then helped raise the initial funds to launch this ministry into reality.

Fourth is my recently departed and dearest friend, Pastor John R. Carlson (1912-2000), who was the closest copy of the Incarnate Logos I have ever met. This humble brother was my faithful counselor and "Barnabas" for twenty years.

And last but not least is my Canadian brother, Victor A. Zacharias. His sound advice, passion for Christ and faithfulness have been inspirations to my soul.

Without the wisdom and counsel of these five men, along with the present board members, I would have certainly run amok years ago!

Finally, I am eternally grateful to those individuals who have undergirded this work with their faithful prayers and sacrificial giving in order to make PTAM a viable ministry and bring this revised edition to fruition.

To God be the glory for the great things He has done.

Richard A. Burr, general director,
Pray • Think • Act Ministries, Inc.

Introduction:
"Go into Your Closet . . ."

Only one verse in the entire Word of God tells us to pray in a particular location. In Matthew 6:6, we are not only told, we are *commanded*, "But when you pray, go into your room [closet, KJV], close the door and pray to your Father, who is unseen."

The word translated "room" or "closet" refers to a place of solitude where a believer "can withdraw and shut the world out and commune with God."[1] It is a place of silent retreat from the world, a place of entrance into the eternal—a *secret closet* where our spiritual lives are strengthened and revived.

It is within the seclusion of our *private* prayer lives that we develop the habits of the heart that change us into the men or women of God whom we were intended to be. My persuasion is this: *One's spiritual life will never rise above the practice of one's private prayer life.* Therefore, it is within this solitude that God refines us, molds us and prepares us to fulfill His purpose for our lives.

An expert sculptor never transforms a block of marble into a masterpiece in a single session. And the work is not done on a public street corner but in the privacy of the artist's studio. In the same way, God uses the private times alone with Him to begin and complete the chiseling of Christian character.

It is not surprising that this instruction concerning the private prayer life is revealed within the Sermon on the Mount, for the basic theme of that passage is the

1

superior righteousness demanded of a follower of the Lord Jesus Christ. This is verified in Matthew 5:20, where the Lord says, "For I tell you that unless your righteousness surpasses that of the Pharisees and the teachers of the law, you will certainly not enter the kingdom of heaven." If anyone brought a righteous indignation to the heart of Messiah, it was the spiritual leaders of His day who portrayed an external piety but tragically coupled it with internal hypocrisy.

In Matthew 5 the Lord deals with external versus internal realities. Jesus speaks of murder as being external, then suggests that anger, which is internal, is also subject to judgment. He talks of adultery as being external but then identifies the lust of the mind as the internal reality of adultery. The theme of external versus internal continues into the next chapter.

Matthew 6 opens with a yellow caution flag: "Be careful not to do your 'acts of righteousness' before men, to be seen by them. If you do, you will have no reward from your Father in heaven." Jesus names three examples of "acts of righteousness," which some call spiritual disciplines, that should be done in secret:

1. Giving to the needy (in *secret*, without fanfare)
2. Praying (in *secret*, in your closet, with the door shut)
3. Fasting (in *secret*, so it may not be obvious to others)

The point of it all? These spiritual disciplines are not to be done before an audience. Those who parade their piety forfeit their reward.

A Lesson on Prayer

Matthew 6:5-8 escorts us into the classroom where Jesus is teaching on the secret closet. Here He contrasts the public (external) prayer of the Pharisees with the private (internal) prayer of a true disciple and the resulting consequences:

> And when you pray, do not be like the hypocrites, for they love to pray standing in the synagogues and on the street corners to be seen by men. I tell you the truth, they have received their reward in full. But when you pray, go into your room, close the door and pray to your Father, who is unseen. Then your Father, who sees what is done in secret, will reward you. And when you pray, do not keep on babbling like pagans, for they think they will be heard because of their many words. Do not be like them, for your Father knows what you need before you ask him.

These dynamic verses teach us where and how to pray, warn us how *not* to pray and promise a reward—not the applause of others but the favor of God—for those who get it right. They encompass a powerful prescription that teaches crucial principles for our private prayer lives.

What Is Prayer?

Verse 5 states, "And when you pray . . ." What do we mean by prayer? Simply defined, prayer is a *dialogue* between God and a believer, both of whom are to be desperately in love with each other. This definition includes both *talking* and *listening* to God.

However, if we are totally honest with ourselves, most of us would admit that many times our prayers are *monologues*—"babbling like pagans" (Matthew 6:7)—in which we do most of the talking and seldom *listen* to His instruction. Think for a moment: *Could it be that what God has to say to you is much more important than what you have to say to Him?* Certainly He delights in our sacrifices of praise and thanksgiving, but for many, *listening to* and *discerning* His voice is almost nonexistent in their communion with the great Creator.

Suppose in a marriage one spouse dominated the conversation—always talking but never listening. Would such a marriage last? Or what if one spouse always carried a to-do list and expected the other partner to always perform? One would be hard-pressed to find love and intimacy in such a relationship. But for some believers, this is the extent of their communion with God.

Who does most of the talking in your prayer life? Is it truly a dialogue or merely a monologue? Before addressing this issue, let's look more deeply into the meaning of prayer.

The essence of prayer is *not* what we can get from God. Prayer is to be *an intimate and personal relationship* with our living God in which the believer comes to want *only what God wants for him*, nothing more and nothing less. This view of prayer speaks of yielding to God's desires by *dying* to one's agenda. Notice that in Luke 9:23 Jesus proclaimed, "If anyone would come after me, he must deny himself and take up his cross daily and follow me." The Lord uses the symbol of the cross, which speaks of death, to emphasize the necessity of *dying* to self. We must build this into our prayer lives *by actually participating in our own funerals on a daily basis!*

Another key word in this verse is *daily*. He did not say, "Take up your cross at the annual prayer conference" but "Take up your cross *daily*." Dying to self is a daily imperative that must be an integral part of our closet time. This requires a daily commitment of time in solitude with a holy God when we acknowledge, "Yes, Jesus, You are Lord and I am Your servant! You are my Master! I only want what You want for me. Won't You grace me this day, O Mighty God, with Your presence and power?"

This is what prayer is all about: not what we can get from God but to have our hearts so radically changed by Him that we come to want only what God wants for us. This definition is central to the success of developing the secret closet of prayer.

This concept of prayer speaks of a lifetime process in which our gracious and patient God weaves His traits into our lives. He does this by peeling our hearts like an onion. He peels layer after layer of scar tissue (i.e., pride, anger, bitterness, doubt, rejection, etc.) that has accumulated over the years, thus hindering us from being all that He intends us to be.

This is referred to as progressive sanctification—being yielded to Him and allowing Him to gently make those corrections that will mold us into His intended purposes for our lives. Though it can be painful, it is this process of peeling and healing that will lead to wholeness of life.

This kind of prayer develops dependence and intimacy with our triune God and leads us to affirm John

15:5, which says that apart from the Lord Jesus we can do nothing. This is the highest expression of prayer as we desire *only* what He wants for us—nothing more, nothing less.

Hypocritical Praying

Continuing in Matthew 6:5, Jesus said, "And when you pray, do not be like the hypocrites." Who are the hypocrites? This word literally means "playactors." The Scribes and Pharisees were acting out, portraying before the masses their piety, their external righteousness, which, when coupled with the hypocrisy of their hearts, prompted the Lord's warning: "Do not be like the hypocrites, for they love to pray standing in the synagogues and on the street corners to be seen by men."

Oh, how they loved to pray before an audience! They would make their way into downtown Capernaum or Jerusalem at Broad and Main Streets where they would have maximum exposure before the masses and then lift up their hands and pray to the God of Abraham, Isaac and Jacob. What was their motivation? It was to impress others, to score "pious points" with the pedestrian on the street and the worshiper in the pew. Notice the guarantee Jesus gives in verse 5: "I tell you the truth, they have received their reward in full." If you pray this way, then you have already received your reward, since you have attempted to impress others with your so-called spirituality. This style of prayer joins you with the hypocrites of whom Jesus spoke and leaves you with the same vacuum that was in their hearts.

The Command

In Matthew 6:6, Jesus teaches His hearers a profound command, the only one in the entire Bible that sets a geographical location for prayer: "But when you pray, go into your room, close the door and pray to your Father, who is unseen."

Notice that this is the opposite of the Pharisees' practice, the reverse of public exposure. The central issue is *solitude* with God. Why is this so critical? Because *there are some things God only shares in secret, and there are some secrets that are only heard in solitude with Him.* When God spoke to Abraham, Moses, Samuel and scores of other Old Testament saints, it was not in a public setting. It was invariably in *solitude* with Jehovah.

The word *room* also implies a "secret and well-guarded place"[2] where one would store his treasures, such as a bank vault. The secret closet is an environment where one can be "undisturbed to avoid distraction, unheard to experience liberty of spirit, and unobserved to avoid ostentation."[3] This is where God does that deep work of sanctification—purifying and preparing us for all that we are intended to be.

The secret closet is off-field discipline that prepares us for on-field performance. It is the place where God builds His character within our hearts. It is the practice of this private discipline that prepares us for the duties and obligations of public life. For this reason, our spiritual lives will never, ever rise above the practice of our private prayer lives.

The Promise

It is amazing enough that a ragged, hungry beggar is granted an audience with the majestic King, but to have Him respond with favor and reward is beyond our comprehension. Yet this is precisely what Jesus promises in Matthew 6:6: "Then your Father, who sees what is done in secret, will reward you." It does not say how or when, but we can be confident that He will bless us, show us mercy and "reward" us.

However, the enemy of our souls, the author of all doubt and discouragement, will do everything possible to make us think that private prayer is wasted time. For this reason, many Christians flag and fail in this most essential discipline of the faith. Is it any wonder, then, that ninety-five percent of the Christians in America are consumed with carnality, as one international evangelist has stated?

I have often thought about what my greatest surprise will be when I go home to be with the Lord. After much pondering, I have concluded that it will be the tremendous power and peace that was available to me through prayer on this side of heaven—and how infrequently I used it!

Jesus substantiates this thought in Matthew 17:21, where He says, "Nothing will be impossible for you," and in Mark 9:29, where he says, "But this kind does not go out except by prayer and fasting" (paraphrase). Satan hates prayer, particularly the "closet life" of the believer. This is why the discipline of the secret closet is so difficult to maintain, for our sinful nature wars against it.

This command of the secret closet is not a command for husbands and wives to pray together. This is not a command for small prayer groups nor for the midweek prayer service. All of these levels of prayer are important and will be examined in the next chapter, but they are no substitute for the secret closet.

Do you have a place that is a special meeting site for intimacy with God? Do you have a place that is holy ground? Do you have a place of solitude? Do you have a secret closet of prayer?

Study Questions

Personal Study

1. Read Matthew 6:5-8 slowly and devotionally.
2. Prayer is one of the most popular topics in Christian publishing; there are literally thousands of books on the subject. What prompted you to begin reading *Developing Your Secret Closet of Prayer*?
3. How does the author define prayer? How is this definition different from the concept you may be used to?
4. What makes prayer hypocritical? How can you avoid praying hypocritically?
5. As an exercise in making prayer a dialogue, spend some time in silent, private prayer asking God questions like the ones below. Wait quietly before the Lord until you receive an answer.
   - Father, what do You think of me as a follower of Your Son? With the Fruit of the Spirit in mind (see Galatians 5:22), how do I measure up?

- How could I improve my prayer life and, in turn, my relationship with You?
- What truth do You want me to learn this day?
- Whom can I serve in Your name today, and how?

6. Think about a place of solitude where you might be able to have your secret closet of prayer. List some of the things you may want to keep there (e.g., Bible, notebook, concordance, hymnal, dictionary, etc.). Also think about your daily schedule and when you can set aside time for prayer.

7. Why is solitude with God so critical? What are its benefits?

8. Meditate on the first affirmation in the Prayer Covenant (see appendix A). Pray for the Lord to help you be faithful to this affirmation.

Group Study

1. Ask members of the group to share why they chose to begin reading *Developing Your Secret Closet of Prayer* and what they hope to get out of the study.

2. Have one person in the group read Matthew 6:5-8. Identify and discuss the locations of prayer that are taught in this passage.

3. Discuss the importance of solitude in prayer. What can we expect when we spend time alone with our triune God?

4. Has reading the introduction to this book changed your viewpoint on prayer? If so, how? Discuss.

5. Do you agree with the statement that "one's spiritual life will never rise above one's prayer life"? Discuss.

6. Has God spoken to you in prayer about a specific issue in your life? Ask members of the group to share experiences of dialogue with God in prayer.
7. Close by reading together the first affirmation in the Prayer Covenant (see appendix A) and praying together for the Lord to bless this group study.

Part 1
Principles of Prayer

Developing your secret closet of prayer is an all-encompassing spiritual discipline. First, it must be distinguished from other levels and modes of prayer. Second, it must be understood in the context of one's daily walk and life goals. Third, it needs to be planned and prepared for. And finally, it must be conformed to the truths of God's Word. This is what these beginning chapters are all about.

1
Praying from the Inside Out

Several years ago while I was conducting a conference on the secret closet of prayer in New England, the pastor of the host church found a unique way to affirm the teaching. He showed me the original handwritten records of their church, dated August 10, 1787.

I was awestruck by what I read, for the character of the congregation was revealed in those historical documents. The church covenant in particular disclosed their reverence and awe for the holiness of God. But what especially intrigued me, and what the host pastor specifically wanted me to see, was the following portion of that covenant:

> You do now solemnly covenant to give up yourself to be a member of Christ's body in this church, engaging, by His help, to walk with them in all the ordinances and institutions of the Gospel. Particularly, you engage to be a faithful attendant on *the duties of the closet,* family and public worship of God, as He hath appointed in His Word. [italics added]

This is the only church covenant I have ever seen that included the practice of the secret closet of prayer as a condition for fellowship! Notice the order in which the ministry of prayer was to be established in the congregation: from the "closet" to the family altar and finally to the congregational setting (the "public worship of God"). Here we have affirmed the principle of *praying from the inside out.*

How do you develop a praying church? You build it from the inside out. In other words, you begin with the individual and move outward to the corporate body. No wonder the Church and our beloved nation experienced such favor in the sight of Almighty God during those formative years. The early American Church was truly a "house of prayer"!

As mentioned in the introduction, there is only one imperative in the entire Word of God that directs us to a specific geographical location of prayer—the *secret closet*—and that is in Matthew 6:6. From this position you build outwardly and sequentially.

Learning how to pray from the inside out requires an examination of the various levels and modes of prayer—and how to implement them. This is essential if we are to fulfill the Lord's exhortation, "My house will be called a house of prayer" (Matthew 21:13).

Levels of Prayer

There are at least four levels of prayer mentioned (or implied) in Scripture:

1. The Secret Closet

The *first* and foundational level is the *secret closet*, or private prayer life, as detailed in the introduction. The power of the Church is generated in this place of solitude with God, in concert with the enabling work of the Holy Spirit and His unerring Word.

2. The Family Altar

The *second* level of prayer is found in Matthew 18:19: "Again, I tell you that if two of you on earth agree about anything you ask for, it will be done for you by my Father in heaven." This image of two praying together is clearly pictured in the *family altar*. Though the context of this passage discusses church discipline, certainly the Lord must have had in mind the necessity of having a prayer partner and/or the husband-wife prayer relationship.

This verse in Matthew is especially significant when coupled with Ecclesiastes 4:9-10: "Two are better than one, / because they have a good return for their work: / If one falls down, / his friend can help him up. / But pity the man who falls / and has no one to help him up!" This should motivate every believer to have a prayer partner and particularly every Christian husband and wife to pray together. In my many years of ministry, including leading a number of couples' retreats, I have never heard of a Christian marriage in which the husband and wife prayed together regularly that ended in divorce.

However, in spite of these extraordinary promises, the surveys I have conducted show that less than one percent of Christian husbands and wives actually pray together. Is it any wonder that there are so many hurting marriages within the Church? Unless husband and wife are praying together, it is difficult for them to be committed to the same vision—to be of like heart, mind and purpose. The family altar builds a oneness in the marital relationship and a team spirit in the family, but couples who are not praying together are apt to find the "family team" to be an illusive dream.

May God help us to rebuild the family altar!

3. Small Group Prayer

The *third* level of prayer is found in Matthew 18:20: "For where two or three come together in my name, there am I with them." This *small group* or *triplet praying* is inserted between two praying together and the public assembly for prayer. Though there are only two or three—the smallest possible group—we have the promise of Christ's awesome presence: "There am I." We can depend on the power and presence of His Spirit with our spirits.

Triplet prayer is graphically illustrated in Exodus 17:8-13, when the nation of Israel encountered their first armed conflict. Moses ordered Joshua to assemble the men and fight the Amalekites with the sword, while he, along with Aaron and Hur, ascended to the mountaintop with the wonder-working staff, which represented Jehovah's power and presence.

As long as Moses prayed with the staff raised, the Israelites were victorious. But when his arms grew tired and he lowered the staff, the Amalekites began to win. To help Moses keep praying, Aaron and Hur held up his arms.

This exemplifies the supernatural power of prayer even among the smallest of groups. Who won the battle—the men of the sword or the men of the staff? Though the sword was essential for victory, the prayers of these three men were the determining factor!

4. Congregational Prayer

The *fourth* level of prayer is found in Acts 1:14: "They all continued to give their persistent attention

with absolute unanimity to prayer which was character-
ized by its definitiveness of purpose, together with the
women and Mary the mother of Jesus and with His
brethren."[1] Here we find 120 disciples of Christ hud-
dled in an upper room, waiting for the descent of the
Spirit upon them. Jesus' promise of the Holy Spirit was
not intended to replace prayer but to quicken and encourage it. As they gave themselves to extraordinary
congregational prayer, coupled with explicit agreement
and visible union, the Dove of the Heavenlies de-
scended upon them with power and grace, giving birth
to the New Testament Church.

This is a graphic illustration of what our Lord Jesus
Christ intended Christianity to be—a way of life in
which the local assembly would be a "house of prayer."
However, when the gospel was exported to the Greeks,
eventually they turned it into a *philosophy*. Then it
emerged in Rome where it became an *institution*. From
there it surfaced in Europe, where it was turned into a
culture. Finally it was exported to America, where we in
this generation have turned it into *entertainment, excitement* and/or *enterprise*.

Tragically, we have failed to realize that prayer is the
launchpad of all ministry and that without it we short-
circuit God's chosen method of work. The prayer service in most American churches has become the least
attended meeting on the church calendar—and in some
cases, the most boring. Many churches have even elim-
inated any semblance of congregational praying.

I am persuaded that these symptoms arise from a
lack of effective *prayer discipleship*—particularly, a lack
of emphasis on the secret closet. How many of us, for

example, remember our fathers, mothers, pastors or any other mature believers taking us aside and actually *teaching* us how to pray? It makes sense that those who do not know how to pray effectively in private will, in all probability, not be inclined to pray in public.

A dynamic praying church must be built *from the inside out*, employing all four levels of prayer: the secret closet, the family altar, small group praying and finally, prayer in the congregational setting. While this book focuses on the secret closet, it is crucial to keep in mind the interrelationship between private and other forms of prayer.

Is your church suffering from prayerlessness? Is it hard to find time and motivation for small group prayer? Are you having difficulty building your family altar? The solution lies behind the closed door of the secret closet.

Modes of Prayer

There are two modes of prayer portrayed in Scripture:

1. Spontaneous

An example of the first and most frequently used, *spontaneous prayer*, is found in the second chapter of Nehemiah. When King Artaxerxes notices the downcast countenance of his cupbearer, Nehemiah, he asks, "Why does your face look so sad when you are not ill?" (2:2).

Nehemiah was indeed sad, for he had received bad news about the Jews who had returned from exile to Jerusalem. The walls of the city were broken down and the gates had been burned, leaving them defense-less before their enemies. Being the righteous leader that he was, Nehemiah had spent many days weeping, mourning, fasting and praying for his fellow Hebrews and their plight. The king had accurately observed the burden of Nehemiah's heart.

Nehemiah responds to the king's inquiry by explaining the condition of the city of his ancestors. This prompts a second question by King Artaxerxes: "What is it you want?" (2:4). Sandwiched between the king's question and Nehemiah's answer, we find the cup-bearer petitioning God: "Then I prayed to the God of heaven, and I answered the king" (2:4-5). This is an illustration of spontaneous prayer, a very useful and powerful mode of prayer. And in Nehemiah's case, it was truly effective, because it opened the door for him to rebuild the walls of Jerusalem.

Most of us engage in this style of praying many times throughout the day. As we shop, we pray that the Lord will grant us a good return for the money we spend. As we visit the family doctor, we plead for grace and mercy. As we walk or jog, we intercede for others as prompted by the Spirit . . . and so on. All of this is categorized as spontaneous prayer.

Several years ago I was asked to share the meaning of Christmas at a friend's home. He had just been converted a few months before, and it was his family's custom to have an annual bash on the Sunday prior to Christmas. Typically their guests (mostly unbelievers) would quite generously indulge themselves with alcoholic drink. His intention was that I give a gospel message centered around the birth of Jesus.

Upon my arrival, my enthusiastic friend greeted me at the door and with much excitement proceeded to inform me of the large number of guests that they were expecting. Then very abruptly he shared a vexing problem: "Do you think we should serve some wine? I realize we shouldn't give them the hard stuff, but what about a little wine? After all, didn't Jesus turn water into wine at a festive occasion?"

Richard, what in the world have you gotten yourself into? I asked myself. But to my friend I said, "Well, Gordon, what do you think you should do?" Immediately he responded, "I think we need to pray!"

With that he ordered me to follow him to his study. When we got there, he gave me another command: "Get down on your knees over there and I'll get down here." Then my friend led in spontaneous prayer.

"Jesus Christ, this is Gordon Walker here, and we have a mess of a problem on our hands. You know these unbelieving friends of mine have no idea what kind of a party they're coming to, and I'm uncertain about serving them wine. The time is short, Lord, so I'm counting on You to answer quickly! Now, Burr wants to talk to You."

At this I doubled over in laughter, for his prayer had all the characteristics of simplicity, sincerity and even a phone line to the throne room of the heavenlies. After regaining my composure, I prayed; then we got up off our knees and hustled out to the kitchen where my friend informed his charming wife that God indeed had answered our prayers—there would be no wine! Instead, they decided to use a counterfeit white grape juice mixed with a couple of other juices, all of which were "unleaded."

It was interesting to watch their friends frequenting the punch bowl—absent the "punch." After a while I was privileged to share the authentic Christmas story. What an experience—and it was all in answer to spontaneous prayer!

2. Designated Times

The second mode of prayer could be labeled *designated times* with God. This is illustrated in Daniel 6:10: "Now when Daniel learned that the decree had been published, he went home to his upstairs room where the windows opened toward Jerusalem. Three times a day he got down on his knees and prayed, giving thanks to his God, just as he had done before." This suggests that Daniel had regularly scheduled appointments to be alone with Jehovah.

This mode of prayer is possibly the most significant because it implies a disciplined commitment to set aside time to be with our great Creator. This mode is applicable to all four levels of prayer. Every Christian should have a designated time to meet with God in solitude, as well as a designated time spent with a prayer partner or a small prayer group. And certainly the midweek congregational prayer meeting would be considered a designated time of prayer.

The secret closet of prayer is a *designated time* to be alone with God. It is in this environment that believers develop intimacy with God. This is where we are revived and molded into the people our Master intends us to be.

It is sad to see Christians who have been in the faith for many years but have never experienced this personal intimacy with their living Lord. The following testimony bears witness to this fact:

This is not so much the story of a man who had sunk so deeply in sin as to bring about much shame upon his family, but an account of a gracious Savior so ready to forgive and stand by a man.

When this man fell upon his knees to acknowledge his transgressions, he learned that this Savior had already washed away his sins and desired to take up residence in his heart. At that very moment he was saved for all eternity!

Did he immerse himself into the Word? Did he become a man who lived off his knees in prayer? He did not. The only thing he did was truly repent and turn from his wicked ways.

This man was then asked to become a deacon. He consented, not having the foggiest notion of what was expected of him. Indeed, God was so patient. Would you believe forty years of patience?

Then this man moved to a new area and another church, where again he was asked to serve as a deacon. Again, he consented, but this time he knew the "ropes"—all the while continuing to test God's patience.

Finally this man was exposed to the teaching of the "secret closet of prayer," along with the powerful dynamic of Scripture praying. Then God said, "Jimmy, no more hiding. No more pretending. No more counterfeit religion."

I'm the man in this story, an eighty-two-year-old man who has found boundless joy in my closet of prayer, who has experienced a new passion for my Savior and abounding love for my brothers and sisters in Christ. By the way, I have been forgiven for all those lean and wasted years!

Oh, how I praise God for reaching into my soul in these winter years of life and introducing me to the secret closet of prayer that has led to a truly intimate and personal relationship with my Lord Jesus Christ!

James Marr (1915-2004)
Island Baptist Church
Camano Island, Washington

This dear brother is an example of what happens when a man or a woman *captures an ever-consuming vision* for becoming a praying saint and sees how it relates to the totality of life. The importance and nature of this vision is discussed in the next chapter.

Study Questions

Personal Study

1. Identify what the author means by "praying from the inside out." Do you think this concept holds true for you, your family and your church? What kind of changes might you see in your family and church if you further developed this concept of "praying from the inside out"?

2. Read Matthew 18:19. The author identifies this verse with the practice of having a prayer partner. Do you have one? If you have a spouse who is a believer, do you regularly pray with him or her?

3. Was the author's concept of a family altar a new idea to you? If you do not currently have this practice in your family, think about ways you could institute it.

4. Read Matthew 18:20. When you pray with other believers, do you usually think of it as gathering in Jesus' name? Do you sense the Lord's presence? How does meeting together in Jesus' name affect the content of your prayers?

5. Read Acts 1:14. This passage speaks of the early Church believers being "joined together" in prayer. The Greek word literally means they had "one passion." What made the first-century believers unified in their passion for prayer? How does this relate to the concept of the secret closet?

6. On a scale of one to ten, with ten being the highest, rate your participation in the four levels of prayer:

Secret Closet	1	2	3	4	5	6	7	8	9	10
Family Altar	1	2	3	4	5	6	7	8	9	10
Small Group	1	2	3	4	5	6	7	8	9	10
Congregational	1	2	3	4	5	6	7	8	9	10

7. Read Nehemiah 2:4-5. This kind of spontaneous prayer is usually a response to encountering a problem or need in the course of an average day. How often do you respond to a life situation with an impromptu prayer? How might you learn to make this kind of response more of a habit?

8. Daniel had a regular practice of praying three times a day, and he continued this practice even when it violated the law and put his life at risk (see Daniel 6). Think about what it would be like to follow his example. We don't know how long

Daniel's times of prayer were, but just for the sake of argument, imagine yourself including three daily prayer sessions of ten to fifteen minutes each into your schedule. Would it be doable? What would you have to give up? Would it be worth it?

Group Study

1. Welcome any new members of the group and ask them to share what they hope to get out of the study. Invite others in the group to share any changes they have seen in their prayer lives since the previous meeting.

2. Discuss the author's concept of praying from the inside out. What would happen if this were implemented in your church?

3. Have the group list family issues about which they might pray with their spouses and/or families. (They may include such things as praise, thanksgiving, salvation of family members, family finances, children's school performance, etc.) Suggest that the members of the group write down this list and use it at their own family altars. (Note: Praying together can be a sensitive issue between spouses, so try to handle this topic carefully, especially if both husband and wife are in the group.)

4. Have someone read Matthew 18:19-20. Have the group break up into prayer partners or triplets and spend a few minutes practicing small group prayer. (Note: Though small group prayer is both common and scriptural, there may be members of the group who have never done it or are

not entirely comfortable with it. It may help to provide the participants with short lists of suggested topics to pray about.)

5. Discuss the two modes of prayer mentioned by the author—spontaneous and designated times. What can help you develop and strengthen these two habits?

6. Read the testimony of James Marr at the end of the chapter. Close in prayer, asking that the members of the group might have the same experience of joyful and enriching prayer.

2
The Ultimate Purpose of Life

Several years ago, the American public was shocked by the television coverage of the Los Angeles riots. It was a classic example of people running wild, without restraint—looting stores, burning cars, smashing windows.

This is the picture that Proverbs 29:18 paints of a people with no vision. The King James Version of this text reads: "Where there is no vision, the people perish." The New American Standard reads, "The people are unrestrained." The Living Bible is more descriptive: "The people run wild."

In this verse the word *vision* implies a God-given revelation—the power of perceiving something not actually present to the naked eye. For the Christian, vision only comes about through the divine inspiration of the Word of God, in concert with the enlightening ministry of the Holy Spirit. When the Word is coupled with this work of the Spirit, only the Lord knows what the end result will be. Only He knows the impact it will have on a single soul or the world at large.

Have you captured a vision for the ultimate purpose of your life? An ever-consuming vision is the only way to grasp the full potential and power of prayer. Believers who have an improper view of the purpose of life invariably have distorted priorities. As a result, they frequently pray for the wrong things: "When you ask, you do not receive, because you ask with wrong motives, that you may spend what you get on your pleasures" (James 4:3).

But there is an even graver danger. Distorted priorities lead to friendship with the world, which ultimately destroys love for God: "Don't you know that friendship with the world is hatred toward God? Anyone who chooses to be a friend of the world becomes an enemy of God" (4:4).

It is essential, then, for us to examine this subject of vision and see how prayer influences and balances our lives' purpose. This is what determines whether we live triumphantly or in defeat, whether we walk in a state of personal revival or pursue carnality, whether we act in obedience to God's directives or take the pathway of selfish ambition.

Selfish ambition was a problem with which I had previously struggled, and much of it began early in my business career after having a luncheon engagement with a very successful entrepreneur. In the course of our conversation, I asked him, "What have you found to be the secret of success in life?"

"Richard," he said, "I'll share a formula with you, and if you put it into practice, I guarantee you'll be successful." Now, keep in mind that I was not a believer at the time.

He grabbed a napkin and wrote the following words:

VISION + STRATEGY + COMMITMENT = SUCCESS

"You begin," he explained, "with a vision for what you want to accomplish in life. By backing it up with a detailed strategy and a personal commitment to fulfill this strategy, you will become successful." Then he drew vertical lines through each *S* in the word *success* to create dollar signs:

VISION + STRATEGY + COMMITMENT = $UCCE$$

I got very excited. This was exactly what I wanted to hear!

Through the influence of this man, I became a disciple of Napoleon Hill and his philosophy of "Whatever the mind can conceive, and whatever I can believe, I can achieve." I lived by that premise; it became the driving force in my life. Every December I would review the past twelve months and lay out my plans for the coming year. Goals consumed me.

Ironically, though I was raised in a wonderful Christian home and attended a liberal arts college with a Christian influence, I never remember being taught the importance of vision. I do not ever recall being asked, "What is your vision for becoming the man of God that He intends you to be?" I had to go into the corporate arena to be challenged with vision—and there I learned the wrong brand of it!

Confrontation with Truth

It wasn't until several years later, while attending a Methodist men's retreat in Florida, that I was finally confronted with the truth. The speaker that weekend was Dr. Bill Bright, founder of Campus Crusade for Christ. Through his teaching on the uniqueness of Jesus' love, the Lord graciously gave me my second birth, which sparked a revolution in my soul.

Once I had this encounter with my Messiah, I realized that the ladder of "$UCCE$$" I had been climbing was leaning against the wrong building and standing on a corrupt foundation. I suddenly recognized the fallacy of Napoleon Hill's teaching: *It was all centered on self!*

Of course, when I became a Christian, I gave that all up—or so I thought. But God still had some truths to teach me about vision—and once more, He used Bill Bright to do it.

In early 1976, while helping to organize an evangelistic campaign in South Florida, I was privileged to escort Dr. Bright to five different gatherings from Palm Beach to Miami. En route to our final dinner meeting after a full day of speaking engagements, I was struck by the freshness of this man of God. So I asked him how he maintained such vigor and focus in the midst of extraordinary activity.

"There are two critical issues that one must always maintain," he responded. "The first is to have an understanding of the ministry of the Holy Spirit. And the second is to have an ever-consuming vision."

I was silent as I pondered his comments, reflecting upon my past training and business experience. In particular my mind raced back to the formula I had been taught early in my business career:

VISION + STRATEGY + COMMITMENT = $UCCE$$

After a lengthy pause, Dr. Bright asked me, "By the way, Dick, what's your vision?"

"Well, Bill," I responded, "you know that I have come from the corporate arena, so I'm hoping we'll have at least 300 pastors with their wives tonight and most importantly that we'll end up in the 'black' and not in the 'red.' "

Then came his piercing retort: "Friend, if that is the extent of your vision, it is only a matter of time until you get wiped out!"

Suddenly my comfort zone was shattered. I thought, *Could it possibly be that I am in the process of perishing and not even aware of it?*

That experience with Dr. Bright was possibly one of the most significant events of my Christian pilgrimage. It forced me to deal with the primary purpose of life from God's vantage point. Certainly, I had a vision for ministry—the "doing," the horizontal dimension of life—but I lacked a compelling and comprehensive understanding of what the Master intended my life to "be"—the vertical dimension of life.

While a vision of what you hope to accomplish in life is essential, it must be preceded by the vision to *be* the man or woman of God He desires you to be. Otherwise all your words, deeds and achievements—as noble as they may appear—have the potential of being wood, hay or straw (see 1 Corinthians 3:10-15).

Believers and unbelievers across the centuries have pondered questions such as:

- Lord, why did You create me?
- What is the purpose of my existence?
- What do You want to accomplish in and through my life?

The answer to these questions is found in the Word of God, which describes the ultimate purpose of life. Knowing and maintaining this vision of life should be a Christian's utmost concern. Those who do not maintain this vision live in self-delusion, which is perhaps our greatest enemy.

Created to Glorify God

A proper vision for the *ultimate purpose of life* begins with our understanding God's reason for creating the

human race. Genesis 1:27 tells us that we were created in the very image and likeness of God. With such a lofty origin, one would logically assume that God had a very special purpose for us—and He did. In the words of the Westminster Shorter Catechism, God's plan for man is "to glorify God and enjoy Him [rejoice in Him] forever" (see Isaiah 43:7, Romans 15:6 and Philippians 4:4).

To glorify God means that one's thoughts, attitudes, words and behavior are pleasing and acceptable to Him. In doing so, we more clearly reflect the image of God and become an instrument of light, visible and easily recognized in a darkened world.

Tragically, God's chief purpose for man was temporarily deflected and seriously diminished when the serpent deceived the first Adam in breaking his allegiance with God. Consequently, sin entered the human race, and man became totally depraved and spiritually dead. As a result, inherent evil was passed on to every child born to future generations (see Psalm 51:5). Sin caused the glory that was naturally due to God to be deflected back to self.

Since this "fall" of the first Adam (man), there has been a raging battle between God and Satan. It is a battle of two opposing worlds: the world as God intended it to be—good; and the world as man, playing God, wants to make it—evil. This battle rages on two fronts: first and foremost, within the heart of every man; secondly, throughout the society in which we work, live and play. The former determines the latter.

The balance of the Old Testament is given to God's raising up a people and His giving of the

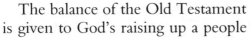

Mosaic Law—all with the intention of showing them their sinfulness (see Exodus 19:4-6) and pointing them to the coming Messiah (see Galatians 3:24).

Despite this deflection and diminution of God's original purpose for man, it has been restored by the second Adam— through the birth, death, burial, resurrection and ascension of our Lord Jesus Christ. Not only did He come to correct the original sin by defeating the Enemy on the cross, but he also came to change the hearts of men and to empower those who anchor their trust in Him to live supernatural lives that are pleasing to God and visible to men.

A Supreme Love for God

For believers who have placed their faith in Christ and who have been grafted into the kingdom of God, glorifying Him would certainly include obedience to His commands. But where does obedience begin? And what is the most important command?

When Jesus was asked this question by the Pharisees in Matthew 22:36-38, He drew upon the great *Shema*, the Jewish confession of faith found in Deuteronomy 6, and answered: " 'Love the Lord your God with all

your heart and with all your soul and with all your mind.' This is the first and greatest commandment."

The question one should ask is, "Do I really have a passion for Christ? Could it be said by the Almighty, 'Yes, this servant loves Me with *all* of his heart, mind and soul'?" If we miss this greatest commandment, it will have a devastating effect on our relationship with our triune God.

This is illustrated in the second chapter of Revelation, where the Lord dictates a letter to the congregation at Ephesus. He commends them for their diligence in duty, perseverance in the midst of suffering and zeal in opposing evil. However, in verse four He declares, "Yet I hold this against you: You have forsaken your first love."

Here was a group of believers committed to doctrine and duty but tragically lax in their passion for the Lord Jesus. Does this characterize your life? If so, the next question is, "How do I rekindle and sustain this supreme love for Christ?"

This could be the most pressing issue in the Church today! The solution, as with any sin, is to repent. But the way to keep that love fresh is to develop an *experiential* Master/servant relationship.

The Master/Servant Relationship

We need to constantly remind ourselves that Jesus is our Master and we are His servants. Jesus tells us in Luke 9:23, "If anyone would come after me, he must deny himself and take up his cross daily and follow me." The phrase "he must deny himself" literally means to disregard one's own interests—the abandonment of self. It does not necessarily mean to assume a passive personality or to deny ourselves certain pleasures but to *yield* to His authority.

The next phrase, "and take up his cross daily," intensifies this principle of self-renunciation. The cross always speaks of death. In New Testament times a condemned criminal was forced to carry his own cross to the execution site as a tacit reminder to the masses that Rome was right and he was wrong, thus deserving of death.

Therefore, when Jesus called you and me to follow Him, He called us to *die*. As I said before, *He has called us to participate in our own funerals on a daily basis.* We must die to our agendas, to our possessions, to our positions in life, and yield ourselves completely to Almighty God *every single day*. This is what following the Master is all about: dying to self and taking the same road that Jesus took as a habit of life—*even unto death!*

Following Jesus, though very rewarding, will cost us everything; and if it doesn't, there is a defect in our understanding of the Master/servant relationship. Our calling is to be the type of servant whom the Bible calls a *bondslave*—one who voluntarily gives himself to a lifetime of commitment and service to the Master. Our only desire should be the will of the Master. For His part, the Master commits Himself to protect, provide and care for *all* the needs of His servant.

Am I really a servant?

Our *only* reason for existence—to glorify God—is the foundation for this ultimate purpose in life. But this deals only with the vertical dimension—our relationship to God. How does this work itself out in the horizontal dimension—our daily living and our relationship to others? And what does all this have to do with the secret closet? The answer to these questions is addressed in the next chapter.

Study Questions

Personal Study

1. This chapter poses the question, "Have you captured a vision for the ultimate purpose of your life?" How did you respond when you read that? Write out a purpose statement for your life in a few sentences.

2. The author gives testimony to how God delivered him from a worldly vision with selfish am-

bition. What was the turning point for him? Was this something you could relate to in your own life?

3. The author shares three questions that believers and unbelievers alike have asked God across the centuries. How do you think God would respond if you posed those questions to Him? Look over the purpose statement that you wrote earlier. Does it answer these questions?

4. Look over the diagrams in this chapter. Which one best illustrates your life at this moment? Which one would you like your life to be like?

5. Read Luke 9:23. In light of this Scripture, what does the author mean when he says that God "has called us to participate in our own funerals on a daily basis"?

6. Spend some time in prayer asking God to show you where in your life you need to die to your own plans, ambitions and agendas and to yield yourself to God for His glory and purposes.

Group Study

1. Have a member of the group read Proverbs 29:18. If anyone has a different translation, ask that person to read the passage as well. Discuss how this verse relates to capturing a vision for the ultimate purpose of one's life.

2. Discuss the concept of writing a purpose statement for one's life. If any group members prepared one for the personal study, invite them to share what they have written and discuss what impact the chapter made on how they worded it.

3. Read Matthew 22:37-38. What does it mean to love God "with all your heart and with all your soul and with all your mind"?

4. What does the author mean by the Master/servant relationship? How does this relate to Luke 9:23, which says that a Christian "must deny himself and take up his cross daily and follow [Jesus]"?

5. Read Galatians 2:20. A paraphrase of this verse would read, "Jesus gave His life for me, in order that He could take my life from me, so that He can live His life through me." Discuss this description of the surrendered life along with the description in Luke 9:23.

6. Close in prayer by asking the Lord for help in loving Him more fully, for dying to self and for an experiential understanding of glorifying God with your thoughts, attitudes and choices. You may want to take turns as a group in saying sentence prayers of commitment.

3
The Horizontal Dimension

Every cross consists of a horizontal and a vertical beam. Both are needed to make a cross, but the vertical beam is the most important, since it always supports the horizontal beam. If the vertical is defective, then the horizontal will collapse.

This same principle holds true for the Christian life. Just as the vertical beam of a cross holds up the horizontal beam, so the vertical dimension of our lives (our personal relationship with God) holds up the horizontal dimension (our relationship with others and our daily walk in the world). If I'm not living as a servant to the Master, if my passion for Christ has eroded, if I'm not glorifying God in word and deed, then the rest of my life is placed in enormous jeopardy.

In the previous chapter, our focus was on the *vertical* dimension of Christian living—*being* the children of God that He intends us to be. In this chapter, we will focus on the *horizontal* dimension—the *doing* of the Christian life.

Love Your Neighbor

As we discussed in the previous chapter, Jesus identified the driving force of the vertical dimension as loving God—the first and greatest commandment (see Matthew 22:37-38). In the very next verse, He lays the foundation for the horizontal dimension: "Love your neighbor as yourself."

Love Your Neighbor

Such a command immediately raises a number of questions, such as:

- How can I possibly love my neighbor as myself?
- Can I do this of my own free will, in my own strength?

It is easy to confuse this command with altruism, a human effort to love without abandoning oneself to God. Such a course is doomed to failure because the vertical dimension is ignored.

The only way that a true, self-giving love for our neighbors can become a reality in our lives is through the experiential knowledge of God's unfailing love for us, coupled with our unhindered passion for Him. It is only out of our relationship with Christ that we can love our neighbors as ourselves.

Walk in the Spirit

Loving our neighbors, however, is not the only thing we are incapable of doing in our own strength. The entire Christian life is an impossible lifestyle. Apart from the empowering work of the blessed Holy Spirit, it is absolutely futile. We must be constantly and conspicuously emptied of self and filled with the Spirit of the Living Christ. Then we can follow the Apostle Paul's advice for daily living: "Since we live by the Spirit, let us keep in step with the Spirit" (Galatians 5:25).

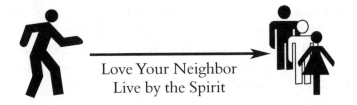

Love Your Neighbor
Live by the Spirit

To determine if you are keeping in step with the Spirit, ask yourself these questions: Is the Fruit of the Spirit, as delineated in Galatians 5:22-23, evident in my life? Is the Holy Spirit ruling and reigning in my life, or have I dethroned Him with self?

The Extension of Christ's Kingdom

When we walk in the Spirit and make visible the invisible Christ, our lives become an animated extension of Christ's love on earth. In other words, one of the most practical ways to love our neighbors as ourselves is to share with them the most significant discovery that we have ever made in our lives: the forgiveness of our sins and the gift of eternal life through the Son of God.

Jesus' last command should be one of our first concerns: "Therefore go and make disciples of all nations, baptizing them in the name of the Father and of the Son and of the Holy Spirit, and teaching them to obey everything I have commanded you. And surely I am with you always, to the very end of the age" (Matthew 28:19-20).

In addition to the Word of God and the ministry of the Holy Spirit, our personal testimonies are one of the most influential resources we have in winning our neighbors for Christ. This personal testimony is made up of our "walk" (the reality of the vertical/horizontal dimensions of our lives) and our "talk" (verbalizing our faith). I am persuaded that eighty-five to ninety percent of Christian witnessing is the "walk" of one's life and the other ten to fifteen percent is comprised of the "talk" of his life.

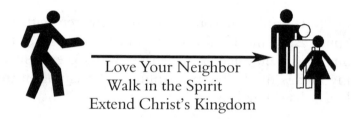

Love Your Neighbor
Walk in the Spirit
Extend Christ's Kingdom

One of the issues in the Church today is that multitudes are praising God on Sunday, but Monday through Saturday they live as something less than righteous neighbors. And the unbeliever sees us and thinks, *If this is what Christianity is, I don't want any part of it. I think what I have is better than what they claim to possess.*

This only emphasizes the necessity of becoming *visionary* Christians, to have an *experiential* understanding of our vertical/horizontal relationships, to be certain that our "walk" is matching up to our "talk."

Destined for the Throne

The final dimension of this *ultimate purpose of life* is that we are destined for the throne! As we live out our lives on this side of heaven, there will come that day, in the not-too-distant future, when either God will call us home or we will experience the second coming of Messiah. This most glorious day is represented by the question mark on the diagram below.

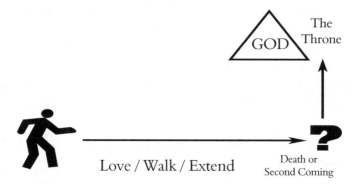

Love / Walk / Extend

Death or
Second Coming

Since none of us knows the number of days assigned to our earthly lives, it behooves us to maintain a balanced perspective by *eagerly anticipating* our ultimate destiny of going home to be with our great Creator and Redeemer while laboring diligently for Him in the meantime. Paul said it well:

> For to me, to live is Christ and to die is gain. If I am to go on living in the body, this will mean fruitful labor for me. Yet what shall I choose? I do not know! I am torn between the two: I desire to depart and be with Christ, which is better by far. (Philippians 1:21-23)

We are bestowed with another promise of grace from the Master Himself, as stated in Revelation 3:21: "To him who overcomes, I will give the right to sit with me on my throne, just as I overcame and sat down with my Father on his throne." This is an awesome declaration in that, while we were yet sinners who deserved death, God not only reached into our lives and delivered us from the dominion of darkness, but He crowns this entire transaction with the blessed hope that we will spend all of eternity with Him! Hallelujah, what a Savior!

To maintain this balanced perspective of life, we must not only recognize from what we have been *delivered* but also for where we are *destined*. The best of all is yet to come!

The Mountains of Life

The word *overcome* in the previous verse means "to gain the victory." We initially "gain the victory" by being redeemed and receiving the gift of eternal life from the Master. However, as we continue to walk this very narrow pathway of life, we find that it is strewn with many trials and tribulations. I like to refer to these as the "mountains of life."

Not only is a "mountain" some trial, affliction or suffering, but in the broader sense it is anything that hinders us from *being* (vertical) all that God desires us to be and from *doing* (horizontal) and accomplishing whatever He has called us to do.

What are the mountains in your life? Is there anything in your life that is hindering you from *being* the man or woman of God that He would have you to be? What is hindering you from accomplishing His purposes in and through your life?

Occasionally, we hit the side of a mountain and "crash." It may be a phone call informing us of the death of a loved one; it may be the discovery that a child is pregnant or on drugs; it may be the "pink slip" in the next paycheck. These are mountains, and sometimes they appear so suddenly and unexpectedly that we crash into them. This, unfortunately, is the reality of life.

But God didn't call you and me to live at the "crash site" on the side of some mountain! He has instead called us to become *overcomers*, gaining the victory, living triumphantly in and through the circumstances of life.

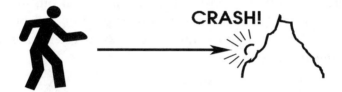

To gain the victory means to face the trial with an unshakable trust in the sovereignty, love, power and mercy of our Lord Jesus Christ—and in the process of this testing to maintain a humble and teachable spirit, knowing with certainty that He will never abandon us. With such an attitude, the very "mountain" that may have been planted by the Evil One to destroy us suddenly becomes the glorious means by which our Savior catapults us to new heights of spiritual maturity and triumphant living. Thus, He gets the glory and we become better equipped to serve our glorious Shepherd.

The Role of Prayer

Here is where our personal prayer lives come into the picture. Prayer becomes a source of power for victorious living. This truth is expressed in the following acrostic:

> **P** rayer
> **R** eleases
> **A** ll
> **Y** our
> **E** ternal
> **R** esources

God has a "warehouse" in the heavenlies for every believer and every congregation. Out of these designated warehouses, with our names inscribed on them, flow all of His eternal resources—everything we need for life and godliness—but only if we become *faithful practitioners* of prayer.

Not only does He release His *power* through prayer but also His *purposes*. This is the wellspring of God-given vision. In addition, He releases His *plans* and strategies, His *peace* and all other *provisions* that we need for living. All of this is accomplished through prevailing prayer.

Prayer, as represented by the two curved arrows in the previous diagram, becomes like a "spiritual umbilical cord," a "life-support system" that conveys nourishment and power from on high. It is through this "supply line" that we draw upon the resources of God and are launched from the "crash site" to soar over the mountains of life, to be led to victorious Christian living and eventually to our ultimate destiny.

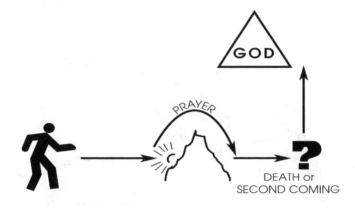

What Is Satan's Response?

The enemy of our souls, the serpent (Satan), will not sit idly by and allow us to live triumphantly. That just isn't his nature. His principal mission is to attempt to neutralize the power, peace and purposes of God by preventing them from becoming reality within our lives. How does he do this? Invariably, Satan's first point of attack is directed at the "life-support system"— the secret closet of prayer. He does everything possible to sever or pinch off this "supply line" in order to render us ineffective and defeated. *The root cause of carnality can often be traced to this very issue.*

In the previous chapter, I emphasized the necessity of grasping and maintaining a *high and holy view of life* as our Master intended it to be. This is vitally important, because Satan's principal goal will always be to neutralize the power of prayer by smothering one's biblical vision for life. The last thing he wants us to have is a *full and experiential understanding* of life from God's perspective.

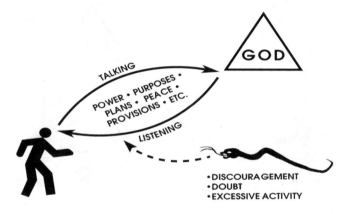

Satan will attempt to smother one's vision in three basic ways:

1. Discouragement

As we travel on this earthly pilgrimage, we are going to have trials. We are going to "hit the side of a mountain"—you can expect it; we will crash. Jesus taught in John 16:33, "In this world you will have trouble. But take heart! I have overcome the world."

Satan will always be right there in the midst of the tragedy, suffering, chaos and confusion, whispering in your ear, "See, your God doesn't exist. And if He does,

He certainly doesn't care about you. You'll never survive this mess. Maybe you should just bail out," etc. This is just like the Evil One. He is truly the *author of all discouragement.*

But as visionary and mature Christians, we don't have to be paralyzed with such deception. We can respond as King Jehoshaphat did when he heard that his enemies were about to attack Jerusalem: "Alarmed, Jehoshaphat resolved to inquire of the LORD" (2 Chronicles 20:3). After dealing with the initial shock of this bad news, he immediately "went vertical"—he purposed to turn the eyes of his heart toward God.

The principle we can learn from Jehoshaphat is to "fix our eyes on Jesus" (Hebrews 12:2), to constantly *gaze* upon God and just occasionally *glance* at our circumstances. Satan will always tempt us to do the reverse—to *glance* at God and *gaze* upon circumstances—which will always lead to discouragement and obscure our vision for life.

2. Doubt

Satan's attack of doubt always begins by questioning the authenticity of God's Word and His existence. If this doubting is not checked, it can lead to the "downsizing" of God, the compromising of biblical values and eventually to unbelief and abandonment of the faith. We are warned in First Timothy 4:1, "The Spirit clearly says that in later times some will abandon the faith and follow deceiving spirits and things taught by demons."

3. Excessive Activity

North Americans live in a culture consumed with a "go-go-go" mentality. Many have their lives set on cruise control in the fast lane of life, entangled in a vortex of activity that eventually leads to weariness of body, mind and spirit. Tragically, this lifestyle has infiltrated the Church; multitudes of believers have allowed their *busyness* to lead to *barrenness* of soul. When this happens, the very first casualty will be their secret closets of prayer, followed by loss of vision and reduction to a level of living that is void of the fruit of the Spirit.

As Christians in an action-oriented society, we must ruthlessly reevaluate our lifestyles. Throughout the Gospels, we never see Jesus in a hurry—we never see Him running down the road, scurrying about or being in haste. But purposeful? Absolutely! He knew what His mission was on planet earth. Our Lord Jesus was truly a *visionary* Servant; He was the perfect model of One who had a balanced and consistent life directed toward fulfilling the purpose of the Father. He knew what He was about!

What's your vision for life? Could it be said by our Lord Jesus that you have a *balanced* and Christ-centered lifestyle? For some, this may seem too abstract, too unearthly. They are looking for a faith that deals with the "real issues of life"—marriage, vocation, family, education, retirement and more.

While these things are important, they are secondary issues—secondary to cultivating an ever-consuming vision for what God intends our lives to be. When we focus on this primary issue, our loving, faithful and infinite Provider puts all secondary issues in their proper place at His appointed time. This is the life of faith that Jesus speaks of in Matthew 6:25, 33: "Therefore I tell you, do not worry about your life, what you will eat or drink; or about your body, what you will wear. . . . But seek first his kingdom and his righteousness, and all these things will be given to you as well."

When someone referred to her blindness as a "tragedy," Helen Keller responded, "Being born blind is not the tragedy, but having sight to see without vision is the real tragedy." Unfortunately, a lack of vision is epidemic among believers. They know *intellectually* that they should seek first the kingdom but have never put it together *experientially*.

The Ultimate Purpose of Life

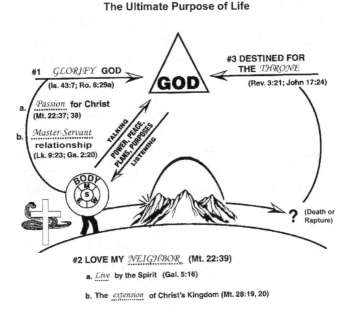

If this describes you, I want to challenge you to take the next two weeks and bury yourself in the content of this chapter. Look up every Scripture and read it in its context, asking the Holy Spirit to give you the proper interpretation. Then begin *applying* it by praying through every verse. If you do this for an hour a day, I guarantee that, by God's faithfulness, you will begin to live in a state of personal revival.

May God so help us to become visionary Christians who have a grasp on this ultimate purpose of life, for "where there is no vision the people perish."

Study Questions

Personal Study

1. Ponder for a moment this statement from the author: "The entire Christian life is an impossible lifestyle." What is the solution to this dilemma?

2. According to the book, what is the difference between loving your neighbor and altruism? Why is it easy to get these confused?

3. Read about the Fruit of the Spirit in Galatians 5:22-23. Which of these characteristics are evident in your life? Which are missing? Pray right now for the Holy Spirit to take full control and display all aspects of His fruit in your life.

4. The author says that our personal testimonies should be eighty-five to ninety percent "walk" and only ten to fifteen percent "talk." What is the ratio in your daily life? Are you more of a walker or a talker?

5. How does focusing on our eternal destiny affect our outlook on life? How does prayer reinforce this perspective?

6. What does the author mean by the "mountains" of life? How do we move beyond such obstacles?

7. The author says that prayerlessness is often "the root cause of carnality" and that Satan uses discouragement, doubt and excessive activity to keep us from prayer. What does Satan use most often to keep you from prayer? How could you ward off such an attack?

8. Perform the suggested exercise at the end of the chapter: Look up every Bible passage from the chapter (2 Chronicles 20:3; Matthew 6:25, 33; 22:37-38; 28:19-20; John 16:33; Galatians 5:22-23, 25; Philippians 1:21-23; Hebrews 12:2; 1 Timothy 4:1; Revelation 3:21) and pray them into your life.

Group Study

1. Begin the session by asking each member of the group to write down a definition of the two dimensions of the Christian life: *being* (vertical) and *doing* (horizontal). Share these definitions with one another.

2. The author defines the horizontal dimension of the Christian life as "loving your neighbor, walking in the Spirit and extending Christ's kingdom." Which of these are you most tempted to do in your own strength? Why?

3. The author reveals that prayer is far more than merely "asking God for things." What are the various aspects of prayer described in this chapter? (If you have a whiteboard available, list these for the whole group.)

4. Read Matthew 6:25, 33. Discuss how "seeking first the kingdom" affects one's day-to-day activities and decisions. (Group members may even be able to share some real-life examples.)
5. Review the diagram at the end of this chapter and discuss the process suggested by it.
6. As a closing prayer, choose one of the Scripture passages listed in the personal study and pray it together as a group.

4
Preparations for the
Secret Closet

What is the most urgent need in the Church today? According to a majority of evangelical leaders across the country, it is revival—a genuine revival of God's people.

By "revival," we do *not* mean a series of evangelistic meetings. The literal definition of the word is "bringing back to life," implying that one has experienced previous "life"—that is, has been born again and had walked in the Spirit—but now desperately needs spiritual restoration. Therefore, *revival is the inrush of divine energy into a believer whose soul is threatening to become a spiritual corpse. It is exclusively the work of the Holy Spirit, in concert with prayer and the Word of God, that restores one's passion for Christ and causes him/her to be flourishing in the fruit of the Spirit* (see Galatians 5:22-23).

The phrase "that restores one's passion for Christ" refers to one's obedience to and passion for the risen Redeemer. Jesus stated it so succinctly: "If you *love* me, you will *obey* what I command" (John 14:15). If I'm not "long" on His obedience, then I will be "short" on His love and in desperate need of *personal* revival!

The late J. Edwin Orr, possibly the foremost church historian on the subject of revival in this century, saw a vital connection between the secret closet of prayer and corporate revival. In his research of revivals and spiritual awakenings, he found that the roots of these movements, if traced back far enough, began with the private prayers of individuals. In other words, corporate revival always begins with *personal* revival—specifically, the revival of one's heart in the secret closet of prayer. The effectiveness of my intercession for family, church and community is directly tied to the spiritual condition of my soul.

Is it possible to walk in a continuous state of personal revival? Yes, but it is costly—very, very costly. It demands radical change in time and discipline. But if you are willing to pay the price, it can produce results that reach far beyond your own life.

The following principles outline the preparations needed to establish an effective prayer life that will lead to personal revival—all by the grace and mercy of our faithful God.

Principle One: Make an Appointment with God

The first and foundational principle in implementing your closet of prayer is to establish an appointment with God. I like to refer to this as the "early morning briefing session."

Years ago I was privileged to fly with Strategic Air Command (USAF), where we engaged in in-flight refueling. It seemed that most of those missions took place in the early morning hours. Prior to takeoff, we would spend a protracted period of time being briefed on the weather, mission objectives, coordinates for refueling points, etc. It would have been unthinkable to go out on a mission without first being briefed by our briefing officer. We would have been court-martialed for such an act of insubordination!

But isn't it interesting how many of us go through our morning routines without spending any time with our Master—our heavenly Briefing Officer—for the "mission" of the day? Yes, we can pray at any time throughout the day, but does it not make good sense to check in with Him before we plunge into our assignments of the new day? After all, who among us apart from the Almighty knows the "turbulence" or the "bandits" (attacks from the Enemy) that we may encounter? Only He knows the phone calls that we will receive, the mail that will come our way and the people who will cross our paths.

Even though Jesus was equal in essence to the Father, He recognized that apart from the Father He could do nothing (see John 5:19). His dependence upon the Father is illustrated in Mark 1:35: *"Very early in the morning, while it was still dark, Jesus got up, left the house and went off to a solitary place, where he prayed."*

On this particular morning, if anyone ever had an excuse for sleeping in, it was Jesus. The previous day, the Sabbath, He had been consumed with preaching, teaching, casting out demons and, after sunset, the healing of the masses (see 1:21-34).

But when the disciples came that morning to the place where He was residing, He was gone. He had risen in the predawn hours, possibly around 5 a.m., and gone off to a *solitary place*, where He communed with His Father.

What did He pray? We don't know for certain, but I imagine His prayers were filled with praise and thanksgiving, along with asking the Father for the "mission plans" of the day. I like to think that He asked, "Father, what is it that You desire to accomplish through Me this day? Where is it You want Me to go?" Such a prayer would make sense, because He did not return to Capernaum where He had experienced successful ministry the previous day but moved on to a new location (see Mark 1:38).

In this brief passage, Jesus modeled a basic and life-giving spiritual principle that we need to embrace and act upon: Our early-morning appointments with God must be a *nonnegotiable* in our daily schedules. If we don't schedule an appointment, in all probability we won't do it. And we must continue to schedule this appointment until it becomes the instinctive response of our souls to gravitate to the closet each and every morning.

Why This Prayerlessness?

Why then is this discipline of the secret closet so difficult to maintain? We could blame it on a myriad of things: laziness, lack of self-discipline, immaturity, excessive activity, physical weariness, etc. However, after searching my own heart over many years, I have come to believe that *self-sufficiency* is the chief cause of this sin of prayerlessness. And, of course, it has its roots in pride—that ungodly arrogance that is spawned in the residue of my old nature, the flesh.

If self-sufficiency is not checked in my life, then instead of drawing on the resources of God, I rely on my own intellect, strength, wisdom, experience, talents and accomplishments. This in turn tears down my faith, trust and dependence in the Lord Jesus Christ.

While instructing His disciples "that they should always pray and not give up" (Luke 18:1), Jesus was deeply concerned with whether He would find them faithfully living off their knees in prayer upon His return. After a stirring promise that God will answer prayer, He raises the question, "When the Son of Man comes, will he find faith on the earth?" (18:8).

What about you? If Messiah had returned this morning, would He have found you in the secret closet, waiting expectantly for His directions for the day? May God so help us to be faithful to that "early morning briefing session."

Principle Two: Select a Location

Jesus gave us the command in Matthew 6:6, "But . . . whenever you are praying, enter into your secret and well-guarded place, and having closed your door, pray to your Father in secret."[1] The primary issue here is solitude, to get alone with God and allow Him to nourish and cultivate your soul.

The place you select could literally be a closet, but a more comfortable location might be some room within your house. Your secret closet could even be your garage, your backyard or your car. The point is to have a *solitary place* where you can be *"undisturbed* to avoid distraction, *unheard* to experience liberty of spirit, and *unobserved* to avoid ostentation."[2]

Why is this so essential? Because it is in this environment, when we are closeted with our Master, that He weaves His character within our souls. It is here that He performs "heart" surgery—peeling our hearts, stripping away all that hinders our relationship with Him and with others. It is in solitude where one can "be still before the LORD and wait patiently for him" (Psalm 37:7), developing a *listening* ear to discern His will, purpose and direction for one's life. There are some things that God only *says* in *secret*, and there are some secrets that are only *heard* in *solitude*.

Our Lord not only commanded us to live in the secret closet, but He personally demonstrated His obedience to this imperative. After completing the miraculous feeding of the 5,000, He dismissed the crowd, instructed His disciples to go to the other side of the lake and then "he went up on a mountainside by himself to pray" (Matthew 14:23). Notice that He didn't mingle among the multitudes but retreated to *solitude* in order to pray.

Another example of Jesus' recurrent practice of withdrawing to a *solitary place* to pray is found in Luke 6:12: "One of those days Jesus went out to a mountainside to pray, and spent the night praying to God." Is it mere coincidence that, after praying through the entire night, He then called for His disciples and took the momentous step of choosing the apostles?

And in Luke 5:16 it says, "But He Himself was withdrawing in the *deserted regions* and was praying."[3] The verb "was withdrawing" is in the present-continuous tense, inferring that this was a regular practice in His life.

It is noteworthy that the deeper our Lord went into public ministry, the more frequently He withdrew to His private practice of prayer. This builds to a climax in

Gethsemane on the night of His arrest. In the Garden (see Matthew 26:36) we have the classic illustration of His electing to be alone with the Father, distancing Himself from His disciples, to work through what was to be the most excruciating event of His earthly pilgrimage. By His actions, He is instructing us that the greater the burden and the more difficult the challenge, the more deeply we should plunge into the closet of prayer.

As one old saint put it, "My present deadness I attribute to want of sufficient time for private devotion. *Oh, that I might be a man of the closet.*"

Principle Three: Consider Your Posture

You can certainly pray in any position: prostrate, standing, sitting, running or kneeling. However, we believe that the preferred posture, if you are physically able to do it, is on your knees, because it demonstrates submission and dependence on the Lord.

One of the tragedies in our society today is the absence of the fear of God. Our culture has become so casual and shameless that strands of this dreadful disease have spilled over into the Church. A *casualness* with God tends toward *carelessness*, *compromise* and *contempt*, which invariably leads to *carnality*. And the posture of your praying can reveal your attitude of heart toward God.

Can a kneeling posture actually *change* your heart attitude? No—but it can serve as an *expression* of your heart, as well as a *reminder* to maintain the right attitude.

In Gethsemane, Jesus modeled this posture of prayer: "He withdrew about a stone's throw beyond them, *knelt* down and prayed" (Luke 22:41). Here the Son of God is not only communicating His dependence upon the Father but also His reverence and submission to Him. Kneeling is an outward expression of an inward attitude of humility and reverence toward the holiness of God. If this was the practice of the Master, it needs to become ours as well.

David exemplifies this posture in Psalm 5:7: "But I, by your great mercy, / will come into your house; / in *reverence* will I *bow down* / toward your holy temple." What does kneeling or bowing before God demonstrate? It demonstrates who needs whom, for He is holy and we are unholy!

On the other hand, Jesus noted that the hypocrites liked to pray while *standing* (see Matthew 6:5). In the parable of the Pharisee and the tax collector, the Pharisee *stands* in prayer—a posture that appears to imply his pride and confidence in himself (see Luke 18:11). Though the tax collector stood as well, it was "at a distance," with his head bowed in repentance (see 18:13). Since Jesus said that the tax collector went home justified (see 18:14), we know that other postures, such as standing, are not wrong, as long as an expression or attitude of humility is maintained.

In Psalm 95:6 we are instructed, "Come, let us *bow* down in worship, / let us *kneel* before the LORD our Maker." Kneeling before God appears to be the more *reverent* and *humble* gesture; it communicates a desperate need for a fresh touch from the Almighty.

A woman came up to me after I gave a teaching on this subject and said, "I just don't see the need of bowing in prayer; after all, I have never bowed before anyone!" Here was a person in need of a cure from the Creator. She was so consumed by her casualness that she was blinded to her carnality! May God draw her to Himself.

Principle Four: Prepare Your Heart

The first three principles that we have just reviewed are *external* preparations that provide a more positive environment for developing intimacy with God. Likewise, there are *internal* preparations that are truly indispensable if we desire to have meaningful and effective communion with our Lord. The following precepts fall into the latter category.

1. Ponder the Throne Room of God

Imagine for a moment that you have just risen from your bed after a refreshing night of sleep and have stepped into your secret closet. You close the door, get down on your knees and, using a bed, chair or table as an altar, you open and lay before you the Word of God. You are alone with your great Creator; you now have an audience with the King of kings!

What's next?

We find that pondering Revelation 4 prepares the heart for an intimate dialogue with our living God. Read and pray through all eleven verses of this brief chapter and you will capture a grand glimpse of the glory that is awaiting you in the throne room of heaven. This is no extra-biblical, mystical teaching but a true picture described by the Apostle John. It is intended to capture your imagination and influence you to take part in this heavenly activity.

What do you see?

The throne is encircled by a rainbow resembling that of an emerald. In front of you, seated on the throne, is God the Father. To His right (and your left, as you look upward) is the Lamb of God—our Lord Jesus Christ, our heavenly Intercessor. Surrounding the outer perimeter of the throne room are the twenty-four elders, fitted with garments of white and golden crowns. High above the throne are the seraphs calling to one another, "Holy, holy, holy is the LORD Almighty; / the whole earth is full of his glory" (Isaiah 6:3).

Picture in your mind the four living creatures, with faces like a lion, an ox, a man and an eagle, positioned around the throne, constantly worshiping the Lord by proclaiming, "Holy, holy, holy / is the Lord God Almighty, / who was, and is, and is to come" (Revelation 4:8). Now join in with these eternal praises from your heart, along with the living creatures, the twenty-four elders and the heavenly hosts, as they bow before the Sovereign One, exclaiming: "You are worthy, our Lord and God, / to receive glory and honor and power, / for you created all things, / and by your will they were created / and have their being" (4:11).

Listen with your heart to the rumblings and peals of thunder; sense the power from the presence of the Almighty; visualize the flashes of lightning coming from the throne and reflecting upon the glassy sea. The setting of the throne room is awesome! Yet even more astounding is God's invitation for us to approach Him with freedom and confidence—all because of the blood of the Lamb! This is affirmed in Hebrews 4:16, where we are invited, "Let us then approach the throne of grace with confidence, so that we may receive mercy and find grace to help us in our time of need."

There at the throne of grace you are privileged to gaze into the majestic and glory-filled face of the Master. He in turn smiles on you and begins to fill your cup until your heart is overflowing with streams of living water—the beginning of the process of *personal* revival.

As you immerse yourself in Revelation 4, capture the vision of this passage. Even though you are on your knees in solitude before God on *this* side of heaven, you are transported into the very presence of the Almighty God through the wonder-working ministry of the Holy Spirit.

Hallelujah, what a Savior! Let it flow, Lord, let it flow!

2. Reflect upon the Eternal View of Life

As you continue on your knees before the throne of grace, allow the Holy Spirit to refocus your view of life through God's eternal perspective (see chapters 2 and 3). All too often we have a limited and distorted view of what God is allowing to take place in our lives. But when we are empowered by the Spirit to see our lives through the eyes of God, we take on a totally different appreciation for how His mercy and grace work through the struggles of life. As we go through trials with God's perspective, we realize that His love endures forever, that He has a perfect plan for us, that He is the Master and we are His servants. We need to become *visionary* Christians by allowing the Master to write this eternal view of life across the tablets of our hearts.

The diagrams in chapters 2 and 3, and particularly the one on page 53, are intended to graphically portray this big picture of life from our Creator's vantage point—and to embrace all the cardinal points of Christian doctrine. Take a few moments every day for the next three weeks to pray through the Scripture passages given in those chapters. Ask the Lord to engrave these truths in your mind. By making this an integral part of your closet time, you will begin to experience a change of attitude and lifestyle much like David expressed in Psalm 138:6-8:

> Though the LORD is on high, he looks
>   upon the lowly. . . .
> Though I walk in the midst of trouble,
>   you preserve my life. . . .
> The LORD will fulfill his purpose for me;
>   your love, O LORD, endures forever—
>   do not abandon the works of your hands.

3. Consider God's Attributes

We are instructed in Psalm 111:10 that "the fear of the LORD is the beginning of wisdom." Therefore, a comprehension of His attributes is essential. Failure to understand the character and attributes of God will undermine the awesome wonder and reverence that is due His name, much like the woman we mentioned earlier who saw no need to bow before God.

There are scores upon scores of attributes and characteristics ascribed to our God, but for our consideration, we will touch on only four of them: His *sov-*

ereignty, omniscience, omnipresence and *omnipotence.* Others, such as His holiness, love, forgiveness, mercy, grace, etc., will be mentioned later.

The word *sovereignty,* as it applies to the character of God, infers that He has the *power* and *authority* to work all things to the good of those who love Him. Therefore, in a certain sense, He ordains whatever comes our way, though He is neither the author of sin nor will He violate our freedom of choice. This is illustrated in Job's life, where Satan could not get to Job without God's permission (see Job 1). By Satan's own admission, there was a hedge (that protective wall of the Holy Spirit) around Job and all his earthly possessions, including his home, family, servants and herds. But built into that hedge was a gate that could be opened or closed—and God was the gatekeeper. What did the Lord do? By His sovereign will, He opened the gate and allowed the pernicious one to plunder Job's possessions and destroy his children.

Job responded by failing to comprehend the Lord's *sovereignty* as it was being worked through his circumstances. He was totally unaware of the confrontation in the heavenly realms between God and Satan. He had no idea that he had been appointed to the lead role of this object lesson. Caught up in his pain and suffering, Job forgot that God has the power to take afflictions and work them to His people's benefit, all the while bringing glory to Himself. Despite Job's doubts, in the end, God not only brought glory to Himself by conquering Satan but He "made [Job] prosperous again and gave him twice as much as he had before" (Job 42:10).

Many of us can readily identify with Job and his troubles, because all too often we have responded in the same way as Job did. This is why having the proper perspective of the purpose of life from the Master's viewpoint is essential. This is why understanding the *sovereignty* of God is so critical. Nothing—*absolutely nothing*—can touch me without passing through the filter of God. And if what I perceive as tragedy does come my way, then I know by faith that my loving, merciful, *sovereign* Lord is going to use it in such a way that it will eventually work to His glory and to my soul's benefit.

How comforting to know that our Lord Jesus Christ has the power and authority to take all the tragedies of the past or present and by His abounding grace turn them into triumphs! May our gentle Shepherd grant us that extra portion of faith to trust Him with the totality of our lives.

We must also recognize that our Most High God is *omniscient*, *omnipresent* and *omnipotent*.

David, in his prayer in Psalm 139, touches upon each of these divine attributes. First he reflects upon God's perfect knowledge, that is, His omniscience. In verses one through three he declares, "You have searched me / and you know me. / You know when I sit and when I rise; / you perceive my thoughts from afar. / You discern my going out and my lying down; / you are *familiar* with all my ways." It is reassuring to realize that our Lord knows everything about us, including our needs, for His knowledge is limitless.

As regenerated believers who have been grafted into the kingdom of God through the blood of the Lamb, we are sealed with the Spirit of Christ (see Ephesians 4:30). He lives within us (see 2:22) and will be with us forever (see John 14:16). Furthermore, we are told in First Corinthians 2:11 that "no one knows the thoughts of God except the Spirit of God."

We have access to the infinite mind of the Omniscient One through the Holy Spirit in concert with the Word of God, for the Word and the Spirit are always in harmony with each other. And one of the principal functions of the Spirit is to infuse our finite minds with the clarity of the truth from on high.

Next, David refers to God's *omnipresence*. "Where can I go from your Spirit? / Where can I flee from your presence?" (Psalm 139:7). The implied answer is, of course, "Nowhere!" The Hound of Heaven will always be with us; we are always under His watchful care (see 139:8-10). How reassuring to know that we are never alone!

Many years ago when I was going through my own "Gethsemane," I was encouraged with an old hymn, "Never Alone." The first stanza reads:

> I've seen the lightning flashing,
>   And heard the thunder roll;
> I've felt sin's breakers dashing,
>   Trying to conquer my soul.
> I've heard the voice of my Savior,
>   Telling me still to fight on;
> He promised never to leave me,
>   Never to leave me alone.
> No, never alone! No, never alone!
>   He promised never to leave me,
>   Never to leave me alone.[4]

Thank you, Lord, that You will never abandon us! The last attribute that David touches upon in Psalm 139 is God's *omnipotence*, that is, His absolute and infinite power. In verse 13, he declares: "For you *created* my inmost being; / you *knit* me together in my mother's womb." Jeremiah reinforces this truth when he observes, "Ah, Sovereign LORD, you have made the heavens and the earth by your great power and outstretched arm. Nothing is too hard for you" (32:17).

We have the privilege of drawing upon the same power that lifted Jesus from the grave. In Acts 1:8 our Lord promises, "You will receive *power* when the Holy Spirit comes on you." And in Second Peter 1:3, the Apostle declares, "His divine *power* has given us everything we need for life and godliness." Unfortunately, we often think of the power of the Holy Spirit as something to use, rather than a Person who wants to use us.

If your time of prayer with the Almighty is to be intimate, personal and life-changing, you must become a student of the character and attributes of God. Prayer was never intended to be some mindless lip labor but a living communion with a holy God that engages the totality of one's intellect, emotions, will and spirit.

4. Satan Is None of the Above!

Satan is not sovereign, omnipotent, omniscient or omnipresent! He is limited in what he can do. He is a conquered adversary. All too often we give him more credit than is due him by not being mindful of who God is. And yet, Satan is powerful, cunning and deceitful, with a singular mission to seek and destroy. In order to know how to triumph over him, we must be mindful of his stratagems. There are three basic ways in which he operates.

The first is by direct satanic attack. This is illustrated in the story of Job (see Job 1-2) and also in the Garden of Eden (see Genesis 3:1-7). But we must be mindful that he cannot be in two places at the same time. If he is in London, he cannot be in Washington. He is not omnipresent!

The second is through evil spirits. He has legions of these spirits around the world. This is his army, which accounts for the wickedness we see throughout society. We are instructed in Ephesians 6:12, "For our struggle is not against flesh and blood, but against the rulers, against the authorities, against the powers of this dark world and against the spiritual forces of evil in the heavenly realms."

The third way in which Satan operates is through the flesh—and this is where most Christians struggle. We must understand that the flesh is the residue of our old crucified nature. And the old crucified nature has its roots in the fall of man as detailed in Genesis 3 and Romans 5:12-21. All the evil we see in and throughout our society is the consequence of that epochal event in the Garden of Eden.

We must keep in mind that our flesh has no fear of God, that it is cunning, deceitful, arrogant and rebellious. The flesh never wants me to pray, never wants me to develop intimacy with God. It truly is a representative of Satan himself.

The Christian's heart, therefore, is like a combat zone where the forces of good, represented by the new nature in Christ, are warring against the forces of evil, represented by the flesh (i.e., the residue of the old nature). There will never be a negotiated peace treaty between the two. This battle will be raging within our souls until God calls us home. This doctrine is confirmed by Paul in Galatians 5:17, where he states, "For the sinful nature [the flesh] desires what is contrary to the Spirit [the new nature], and the Spirit what is contrary to the sinful nature. They are in conflict with each other, so that you do not do what you want."

Which one—the flesh or the Spirit—is winning the battle in your life? The answer is whichever one you feed the most!

Principle Five: Submit to God, Resist the Enemy

The secret to winning the battle is found in James 4:7: "Submit yourselves, then, to God. Resist the devil, and he will flee from you." This is possibly one of the most significant Scriptures in the entire Word that deals with victorious living. On the surface it looks very simple, but in reality it can be very challenging. There are five steps to this:

1. Express Your Desire to Worship and Serve God Only

You and I are confronted every morning with a decision that will determine the outcome of our day. It is the conscious acknowledgment before God that the desire of our hearts is to worship and serve Him throughout this coming day. Why is this essential? Because the flesh has a different agenda. Its natural tendency and mission is to create doubt, discouragement, spiritual indifference, love for the world and self-sufficiency, rendering us ineffective in serving God.

This truth is illustrated in Jesus' temptation in the desert:

> Again, the devil took him to a very high mountain and showed him all the kingdoms of the world and their splendor. "All this I will give you," he said, "if you will bow down and worship me."
>
> Jesus said to him, "Away from me, Satan! For it is written: 'Worship the Lord your God, and serve him only.'"
>
> Then the devil left him, and angels came and attended him. (Matthew 4:8-11)

This is the strongest rebuke used by Jesus against Satan. He did not enter into some lengthy diatribe but simply gave the command, "Away from me, Satan!" Then He reached into the resources of His heavenly Father and spoke the Word of God, from Deuteronomy 6:13, to the devil: "For it is written . . .".

Notice the results: "Then the devil left him." As disciples of Messiah, we must learn from Him how to respond to satanic suggestions. All too often we are tempted to stand toe-to-toe with the devil, shouting, fussing, arguing and giving him too much attention. This kind of response is not seen in Scripture; we must model Jesus!

As you gravitate to the closet, prepare your heart by praying something like, "O Lord, as I arise this morning, I give You my first waking thoughts, for it is my desire to worship You and serve You exclusively throughout this coming day."

2. Voluntarily Submit to His Authority

Not only are we to express our desire to worship and serve Him, but we must yield to His authority. James 4:7 contains a double command (submit and resist) followed by an incredible promise (the devil will flee). In order for the promise to be activated, it must be preceded by one's obedience to both of these commands.

The first command states, "Submit yourselves, then, to God." I believe that much of our victorious living pivots on our obedience to this imperative. Tragically, many Christians despise the "S" word, because it means surrender—to yield to a higher authority. For those of us who live in North America, the word *surrender* is absent from our cultural vocabulary. But to the followers of Jesus, the "S" word is absolutely essential for victorious living. What a contrast from the world! In Christ's kingdom you must submit in order to triumph.

Our Lord identifies submission as a condition for discipleship in Luke 9:23: "If anyone would come after me, he must *deny* himself and take up his cross daily and follow me." The term *deny* does not so much refer to the giving up of certain foods and pleasures as to the complete submission to the Lordship of Christ, relinquishing all rights and authority to one's life.

The Lord shows us how to deny self by adding, "And take up [your] cross daily and follow me." We must understand that the cross always speaks of death and separation, never of compromise. Here, Jesus is not instructing us to carry our burdens. On the contrary, He speaks of the necessity of dying to self and yielding to Him on a daily basis. In other words, we are called to daily participate in our own funerals, to consider ourselves dead unto the world and alive unto Christ.

Again, we return to the definition of prayer. The goal is not what we can get from God but to have such an intimate and personal relationship with Him that we come to want only what He wants for us—nothing more and nothing less. This definition, in and of itself, speaks of the necessity of dying to self and submitting to His will.

The Apostle Paul certainly understood this truth of the crucified life when he stated, "I have been crucified with Christ and I no longer live, but Christ lives in me. The life I live in the body, I live by faith in the Son of God, who loved me and gave himself for me" (Galatians 2:20).

How then do we personalize this in prayer? In addition to acknowledging our desire to worship and serve Him only, we now add to that prayer something like this: "Lord, this morning I present myself as a living sacrifice to You. I desire only what You want for me. Therefore, I die to all my possessions [name those that come to mind], to all my positions in life [name those that come to mind], and by so doing I yield to Your authority and direction through my life this day. Make me a bondslave to your will."

3. Acknowledge Your Dependence upon Him

On the night of His arrest, Jesus gave His disciples specific encouragements to comfort their souls, for His departure was imminent. Included in this discourse was the subject of fruitfulness—that is, His followers bearing spiritual fruit in their lives (see John 15:1-17). And in the midst of His instruction, He made a most startling declaration: "Apart from me you can do nothing" (15:5).

Now, most of us believe this intellectually, but what about experientially? Is this demonstrated in our actions? Personally, I must constantly remind myself of this truth. For this reason, I incorporate into my prayer time each morning something like, "Lord, as I present myself to You as a living sacrifice, as I die to self, I once again acknowledge that apart from You, I can do absolutely nothing! Therefore, I drive another nail into the coffin of my flesh this morning, trusting that You will have full sway in my life this day."

Praying in such a way reinforces our submission to God and prepares us to be used by Him.

4. Express Your Desire to Live a Spirit-Filled Life

The Spirit-filled life is a life surrendered to the majesty, glory and authority of our Lord Jesus Christ. It is a life empty of self, cleansed and full of the Spirit. This is where the second command of James 4:7, "Resist the devil," comes into play.

How can we "resist the devil"? In and of ourselves, it is impossible. But, as we live in obedience to the first command in James 4:7, "Submit yourselves, then, to God," the Lord empowers us to "resist the devil." The Holy Spirit desires to rule and reign in our lives and to provide us with all the power necessary to live triumphantly. When this transaction takes place, we draw upon the same power that raised Jesus from the grave, that supernatural power of the Holy Spirit. This power is not something for us to use, but it is Someone—a Person who wants to empower us for His use.

As we are empowered by the Spirit, we are prepared to take our stand against the Evil One and resist the best he can hurl against us. Then we will see the fulfillment of the promise in James 4:7, "and he will flee."

How then would I implement this into my early morning prayer? "Lord, as I have presented myself to You as a living sacrifice, I now ask that You, Spirit of Truth, would search and convict me of any unconfessed sin in order that I may be a clean vessel. [Pause and take time for this.] I ask You to rule and reign within me. Revive, empower and enlighten me that I may bring glory to You and be a light in the midst of darkness. You know the arena of conflict that I am about to enter. Please hedge me in, for I sense I'm on the verge of overthrow. O God, take control! For the sake of Your name, rebuke the accuser."

This is biblical praying, and we need to exercise it daily.

5. Ask the Holy Spirit to Guard Your Mind

A common problem that many of us have in prayer is the tendency of the mind to wander. But I've noticed that whenever I'm engaged in conversation with a friend, seldom does this take place. What is the cause of this drifting of the mind? I am persuaded that it comes from the flesh. The heart is the very center of a person, from which all thoughts, attitudes and affections flow. Therefore, our flesh fills our minds with chaos and confusion, for it never wants us to have any meaningful communion with God.

The corrective action for this problem is asking the Holy Spirit to guard and hedge your mind. In Philippians 4:7 we are instructed, "And the peace of God, which transcends all understanding, will guard your hearts and your minds in Christ Jesus." Also, in Second Corinthians 10:4-5, the Apostle talks about the weapons of spiritual warfare that we have at our disposal. He implies that these weapons of prayer and the Holy Spirit "have divine power to demolish strongholds" and that they have the capacity to "take captive every thought to make it obedient to Christ."

So, in my early morning time, I pray something like the following: "Spirit of the Living God, I ask You to take captive my mind by hedging me in and protecting me from the wicked influences of my flesh. Cause my mind to be quickened, focused and centered upon Christ. Embolden my faith, give me ears to hear and grant me the courage to obey whatever Your instruction may be this day."

A fundamental truth in prayer is the sufficiency of the Word of God, along with the enlightening work of the Holy Spirit. This must be the foundation of one's prayer life. And when this is coupled with both the external and internal preparations, it will lead to quality time with our Lord. May God grant us the strength and self-discipline to put these truths into practice!

The relationship between prayer and the Word of God is crucial. A practical method of Scripture praying is discussed in the next chapter.

Study Questions

Personal Study

1. The author says that revival may be considered the most urgent need in the Church today. How does this relate to the secret closet of prayer?

2. What is the reason for having a time of prayer first thing in the morning? If this is not your current practice, what would you have to do to institute it?

3. Read Psalm 37:7. Why is solitude so critical in prayer?

4. Practice praying while standing, sitting and kneeling, if you are physically able to do so. Which posture best reflects a lowly attitude in prayer? Do you find that kneeling serves as a reminder to you to be humble before God?

5. How do you prepare your heart for prayer? Try the author's suggestions (i.e., ponder the throne room of God, reflect on the eternal view of life, consider God's attributes and recognize Satan's limitations) and see how they affect your prayer time.

6. Begin a time of prayer by practicing the author's fivefold plan for submitting to God and resisting the devil (i.e., express your desire to worship God alone, submit to His authority, acknowledge your dependence on Him, express a desire to live a Spirit-filled life and ask the Holy Spirit to guard your mind while you are praying). What was the result?

7. Meditate on the second affirmation in the Prayer Covenant (see appendix A). Pray for the Lord to help you be faithful to this affirmation.

Group Study

1. The author says that prayerlessness is rooted in an attitude of self-sufficiency. Discuss how this

attitude hinders our prayers and what we can do to combat it.

2. The author contends that "there are some things that God only *says* in secret and some secrets that are only *heard* in solitude." Do you agree with this statement? Discuss.

3. The author warns that "casualness" toward God, especially in prayer, is a grave danger. Do you agree? Do you think that kneeling in prayer is important? Discuss.

4. Read the author's four suggestions for preparing one's heart for prayer (see number five under the personal questions above). How important do you think this heart preparation is? Why?

5. Read the author's fivefold plan for submitting to God and resisting the devil (see number six under the personal questions above). How does this plan help a praying believer fight the dangerous attitude of self-sufficiency?

6. Close by reading together the second affirmation in the Prayer Covenant (see appendix A) and praying together for the Lord to help you maintain a daily appointment with God.

5
Scripture Praying

Several years ago I was privileged to speak at the Greek Evangelical Bible Conference in Leptokaria, Greece, located on the beautiful Aegean Sea at the foot of Mount Olympus. During this five-week period of ministry, God in His providence allowed my life to intersect with a beautiful (both inwardly and outwardly) Greek woman, Anastasia Ioannidou, who was the director of nursing at a mission hospital in Thessaloniki.

After a few months of courtship, along with much prayer and counsel, I sensed that the Lord was calling us together to be husband and wife. I remember so vividly that New Year's Eve when I asked her to marry me. Naturally, it was an emotionally charged time with much rejoicing over the thought of our spending the balance of our earthly lives together. But after many tender moments, she responded with an answer I never expected: "Richard, for me to marry you I must have a Word-oriented command from God that this is His will and not just mine or yours."

I must confess that I was somewhat startled by her answer. But after much conversation we committed this to the Lord, asking Him to speak to us—particularly to her, for I was certain that God was in this!

Anastasia had three major questions that needed God's affirmation:

1. Was her ministry to her own people over?
2. Who would care for her elderly mother?
3. Was I God's man for her?

Obviously, these were very serious and legitimate concerns; if we made the wrong decision, there could be catastrophic consequences.

Fortunately, she had developed the practice of systematically praying through Scripture, particularly the Psalms. So, it was only natural for her to lay those issues before God and wait patiently for His direction. This process of Scripture praying had made her mind so consumed with the Word and her heart so attuned to the Holy Spirit that when God gave His answer, she would know with certainty that He was speaking directly to her without the fear of deliberately taking the Word out of context to satisfy personal ambition.

Over the next sixty-eight days my constant question to her was, "Has the Lord spoken to you yet?" And her answer would invariably be, "No, but I sense He will answer soon." I tried to convince her that His silence indicated His affirmation, but her resolve was steadfast. "No, we must wait for His direction."

Finally, on March 9 I received the phone call for which I had been anxiously waiting. "Yes, yes, Richard! The Lord has heard my request and has answered my questions by speaking through His Word. I will marry you!"

She then proceeded to explain how she had been praying through Psalm 45 that very morning, and when she got to verses 10 and 11, the answers were given:

Listen, O daughter, consider and give ear:
Forget your people and your father's house.
The king is enthralled by your beauty;
honor him, for he is your lord.

Note that all her questions were answered in those two verses: 1) Her ministry to her people was finished; 2) He would provide and care for her mother; and 3) I was the man to be her husband. That answer affirmed for us the second most important decision we have ever made in our lives—the first being our respective decisions to acknowledge Christ as Savior and Lord of our lives.

I share this personal illustration as an introduction to what I believe is the most powerful way that one can pray: Scripture praying. It is truly the perfect method of prayer!

Scripture praying is the practice of using God's Word as the foundation for our communion with Him. The Word and prayer are inseparable. When one engages in prayer without the Word, it can lead to mysticism; when the Word is used without prayer, it can lead to legalism, intellectualism and coldness of heart.

I recall a well-known pastor teaching on prayer and making the following disclaimer: "I am sophisticated in doctrine, but I am superficial in prayer." Scripture praying neutralizes this potential danger by placing equal emphasis on both the Word and prayer. Among the numerous reasons for praying this way are four principal benefits which make up the acrostic P-R-A-Y.

P Is for Purposes

Engaging in Scripture praying always brings you face-to-face with the purposes, priorities and goals of the Almighty. It exposes you to His will. Our Lord's core values are always folded into His Word, forming His nonnegotiable message to mankind. This message, when prayed through, leads you away from self-centered and superficial praying by directing you into the central purposes of our perfect God.

For example, you may be questioning the extent of your relationships with nonbelievers. If you happened to be praying through Psalm 1, you would discover in the first verse the blessing that comes from limited association with sinners: "Blessed [spiritually prosperous] is the man / who does not walk in the counsel of the wicked / or stand in the way of sinners / or sit in the seat of mockers." By internalizing and applying this instruction, the petitioner will be led in the direction preferred by the Master.

Scripture praying is like using the Word as a "road map" for our pilgrimage here on earth. As regenerated believers, we know that our ultimate destination is heaven; however, it is the decisions and directions between here and there that give us concern. As we pray through the Word, it not only guides us through these uncertainties, but it also brings our value system into harmony with the perfect will of God. All this makes the quality of our ride to heaven most pleasant, in spite of a little turbulence along the way.

R Is for Rhetoric

Rhetoric (the proper use of speech or language) is another area of concern when it comes to prayer. How do I address a holy God? What words do I use to express my desires and concerns without compromising the holy reverence He deserves? Many times our prayers become short-circuited because we ask wrongly. James verifies this: "You ask and do not receive, because you ask amiss" (James 4:3, NKJV). Scripture praying allays this fear by allowing the believer to commune with the Lord through the words in which He has chosen to speak to us—the Bible.

We mentioned before that prayer is intended to be a dialogue—that is, talking and listening to God—not just a monologue. Through Scripture praying, we not only use His Word to properly format our prayers, but this same Word is used by God to nourish, encourage and instruct our souls. The Word of God is living and active; it pierces and quickens one's heart; it exposes and judges our thoughts and motives; it lays bare our hearts in preparation for becoming pure; it prepares us to become recipients of His mercy and grace (see Hebrews 4:12-16). It is absolute truth, and by using it properly we will not ask amiss.

A Is for Attributes

When you practice Scripture praying in your devotional time, it constantly exposes you to the *attributes* and *characteristics* of God. By praying through and focusing on these true representations of His divine nature, you will grow in the knowledge of God and develop intimacy with Him.

Even though we will never come to a perfect comprehension of God on this side of heaven (see Romans 11:33), we can develop a personal and intimate relationship with Him. This is accomplished by immersing our minds in Scripture, for it is through the Word that God has chosen to reveal Himself to man.

In the Psalms alone there are more than 200 different attributes and characteristics ascribed to His name. For example, the unfailing love of God is mentioned twenty-six times in different settings and contexts. If you struggle with the thought of whether or not He loves you, consistently praying through the Psalms would lead you to the assurance that His love is infinite and unfailing. This assurance opens the door for a stronger, more intimate relationship with the Lord.

Y Is for Yoked

Practicing Scripture praying also causes you to become *yoked* with the great saints of the faith. Praying through their letters and prayers helps you identify with their struggles and celebrations of life. And from them can be gleaned truths, principles and methods that will enhance your relationship with the Almighty. Over time, this leads to imitating their lives. As the writer of Hebrews instructs us, "Remember your leaders, who spoke the word of God to you. Consider the outcome of their way of life and *imitate* their faith" (Hebrews 13:7).

In essence, by praying through the Word, we take these ancient writers of the Old and New Testaments into the closet with us, and they actually disciple us in prayer through their writings. And in the process we come to reproduce their passion, praise and perseverance in our prayers.

Also, we must be mindful that we are to be yoked with our Redeemer. This means that we are to live in joyful submission, not reluctant surrender, to His authority. All too often we resist His *yoke*, thus forfeiting His promised rest. The Lord exhorts us in Matthew 11:28-30:

> Come to me, all you who are weary and burdened, and I will give you rest. Take my yoke upon you and learn from me, for I am gentle and humble in heart, and you will find rest for your souls. For my yoke is easy and my burden is light.

By praying through Scripture I am constantly reminded of my position in and with Christ: I am a child of the King; He is my Master, and I am His servant. And by His grace I will grow into His likeness.

Observe, Interpret, Apply

Whenever we use Scripture, we should be concerned to arrive at its proper meaning. Even the most sincere believers can mishandle the Scriptures if they don't practice discernment. All too often, careless observations lead to faulty interpretations and improper conclusions. This can be avoided by a simple three-step process: *observe, interpret, apply.*

1. As you pray through Scripture, *observe* the context and to whom it is written. Try to "climb into the skin" of the writer and see the scenes and personalities through his eyes. Take note of the words, phrases and sentences—what they are saying and to whom they are directed.

2. Next, through the enlightening work of the Holy Spirit, *interpret* the text by determining what the writer specifically meant in this historical setting and for what purpose. At this point, we are not interpreting

the Word for our personal use but are looking at it from the author's viewpoint.

3. Finally, after observing and properly interpreting the Word, *apply* it personally by allowing the Word and the Spirit to formulate your thoughts, shape your prayers and determine your actions.

The following illustrates the concept of Scripture praying by using selected verses from Psalm 25.

The Word:

> To you, O LORD, I lift up my soul;
>   in you I trust, O my God. . . .
> No one whose hope is in you
>   will ever be put to shame.
>   (25:1, 3)

Prayer:

> *Father, this morning I lift up to You my mind, emotions and will—the totality of my being. It is in You that I anchor all my trust, hope and faith. Thank You for this incredible promise that as I place all my hope in You, I never will be put to shame!*

The Word:

> Show me your ways, O LORD,
>   teach me your paths;
> guide me in your truth and teach me,
>   for you are God my Savior,
>   and my hope is in you all day long.
>   (25:4-5)

Prayer:

> *Lord, cause me to be conscious of Your guidance as I en-counter multitudes of choices throughout this coming day.*

You know the issues that are before me. Help me maintain the upward look, that my eyes will see the paths that You have ordained for me. Be my Mentor and Guide and grant me a teachable spirit to follow Your designs for me this day. Again, I acknowledge that all my faith, trust and hope are placed in You, for apart from You I can do nothing.

The Word:

Remember not the sins of my youth
    and my rebellious ways;
according to your love remember me,
    for you are good, O LORD.
    (25:7)

Prayer:

Lord Jesus, I praise You and thank You for enduring that excruciating pain and shame at Calvary for my past, present and future sins. Thank You that I'm a forgiven saint by Your shed blood. So, may You always remember me according to Your unfailing love and not by my failures and rebellious ways. Therefore, I praise You and thank You for Your unmerited grace. Thank You for Your divine forgiveness and the grace You give me to extend it to others.

Have you caught the concept and simplicity of this style of praying? Then try it out yourself—go to your closet and apply these truths by praying through David's entire prayer in Psalm 25.

When you engage in Scripture praying, you can be certain that the Word and the Holy Spirit are *always in harmony with each other . . . never in opposition.* For the Spirit rides best in His own "chariot" (i.e., the Word of God). And one of the principal functions of the Holy

Spirit is to take the truth of God's Word and providentially instruct, guide, convict and nourish your soul and to meet your present needs. If your heart's desire is to truly worship and serve Him, this method of praying will always lead you into the will of God. It eliminates the staleness of rote praying as it illuminates your mind with nuggets of biblical truth that you may never have discovered before. Scripture praying will also create a hunger within your heart to plumb the depths of God's Word. For a daily Scripture praying schedule, see appendix B.

The chapters that follow discuss the various elements of prayer and how they can enhance and transform your communion with the living God and lead to the revival of your soul.

Study Questions

Personal Study

1. Write down and meditate on the following statement: "Prayer without the Word can lead to mysticism; the Word without prayer can lead to legalism, intellectualism and coldness of heart." In which of these two areas—prayer or the Word—do you need to develop the most?
2. How can praying through the Word bring your value system in line with God's? Look for a

Scripture passage that challenges you ethically or morally and pray through it.

3. Read James 4:3. Do you ever feel like you are "asking amiss" when you are praying? How does Scripture praying alleviate this concern?

4. The author suggests praying through the Psalms on a regular basis. Read a few of your favorite psalms and identify passages that could be the basis for specific prayers. What attributes of God are found in these passages?

5. What biblical writer do you most identify with or admire? Search through his writings for prayers he prayed or passages that could form a basis for prayer. Use the "observe, interpret, apply" study method mentioned in this chapter.

6. Meditate on the third affirmation in the Prayer Covenant (see appendix A). Pray for the Lord to help you be faithful to this affirmation.

Group Study

1. Begin by asking members of the group to define Scripture praying. Invite them to share experiences they have had with Scripture praying or specific passages that they have used as a model for their prayers.

2. The author says that praying through Scripture is like using the Bible as a road map for life. What do you think he means by that? Discuss.

3. Have someone read Hebrews 4:12-13. How does the Word judge our thoughts and attitudes? How does this relate to our prayer lives?

4. Choose a passage of Scripture, in the Psalms or elsewhere, that speaks about God. As a group,

identify various attributes of God from the passage. What do these attributes mean for our relationship with the Father?

5. Read Hebrews 13:7. What does the writer of Hebrews mean by "imitating" the faith of those who have gone before us?

6. Have the group search through Hebrews 11 for examples of faithful actions that they could imitate in their own lives. Review the "observe, interpret, apply" study method suggested by the author.

7. Close by reading together the third affirmation in the Prayer Covenant (see appendix A) and praying together for the Lord to help you learn to pray through the Scriptures.

Part 2
Elements of Prayer

Just as there are different levels and modes of prayer, there are also different elements of prayer. When properly applied, these elements can give balance and power to your praying. But more importantly, they can enhance your living communion with God, enlightening, encouraging and challenging you to draw near to Him and experience "times of refreshing . . . from the presence of the Lord" (Acts 3:19, KJV).

These elements are:
- Petition (personal requests)
- Praise
- Thanksgiving
- Confession with repentance
- Intercession (prayer for others)

As you review these elements, allow the Spirit of Truth to search and probe for any inconsistency or imbalance in your prayer life. Believers who become consumed with any one of these elements at the expense of the others eventually develop inconsistencies in the "walk and talk" of their lives. For example, some only engage in intercessory prayer with very little praise and thanksgiving. They may give an outward appearance of piety, but inwardly there is barrenness of soul.

The remaining chapters will cover the first four elements—petition, praise, thanksgiving and confession with repentance. Intercession (the privilege of praying for the needs of others), as important as it is, will not be covered in this book because of its voluminous material and because our focus is upon those elements that are necessary for initiating and sustaining personal revival.

6
Petition

As a young believer, I was taught that you never pray for your personal needs until you have exhausted your prayers for others. Over the years I've come to realize the fallacy of this teaching. If intercession is not preceded by the constant nourishing of your heart, eventually your prayers will become cold and answers will be few.

The effectiveness of our prayers for others is directly tied to the spiritual condition of our own souls. If there are "unresolved issues" (sin) within the heart of the *pray-er*, how can God be expected to listen and bring change to the *pray-ee*? Psalm 66:18 clearly states, "If I had cherished sin in my heart, / the Lord would not have listened."

The most valuable possession we have is our souls, and our primary concern should be for their well-being. "What good will it be for a man if he gains the whole world, yet forfeits his soul?" Jesus asked. "Or what can a man give in exchange for his soul?" (Matthew 16:26). The health of our souls determines not only our relationship with God and man but also the effectiveness of our prayers for others. If intercession is to be powerful, it must be launched from a *pure heart*, otherwise our prayers never make it through the ceiling!

This is why the first element of prayer is personal petition.

An Outline for Biblical Prayer

Augustine, in the fifth century, taught the following on the Lord's Prayer:

> If you had a case in court and you wished to present a petition to the Emperor, you would consult a learned man, skilled in the law, and ask him to compose the petition for you; lest, perhaps, you approach the throne in some manner other than the approved one, and not only fail to obtain your request, but be considered worthy of censure rather than favor. When, therefore, the apostles wished to make a petition and were not sure how to approach Almighty God, they said to Christ, "Lord, teach us to pray." That is to say: "You, our Advocate, our Lawyer, our Associate Justice with God, You draw up our petition for us." And from the Book of Heavenly Law, the Lord taught them . . . how to pray.[1]

In essence, the Lord's Prayer is one of petition, and its content is not so much for our instruction *about* God as it is for the construction of our petitions *to* Him.[2]

Petition can best be defined as *an earnest request for one's personal needs.* Since our personal needs consist of spiritual, emotional, physical and material needs, we face the challenge of prioritizing these needs and then presenting them at the throne of grace consistent with our Lord's teaching. How do we decide what is most important?

The Lord gives us an answer to this dilemma in His Sermon on the Mount: "But seek first his kingdom and his righteousness, and all these things will be given to you as well. Therefore do not worry about tomorrow" (Matthew 6:33-34). Our *spiritual* needs must be our chief priority, for we have the assurance that *all other* needs will be providentially met.

The Lord's Prayer gives us an outline of those elements that should be included in our petition to God. Again, Augustine put it well: "Whoever says anything in prayer that finds no place in that Gospel prayer is praying in a manner which, if it be not unlawful, is at least not spiritual."[3]

Let's look at the eight different parts of this prayer as recorded in Matthew 6 (my translation[4]):

"Our Father in Heaven . . ." (Verse 9)

The Lord begins by instructing us to direct our prayers to our heavenly Father, not to saints or angels but to Him who is our great Architect. In other words, if you were to construct a letter to the triune God, the *salutation* would be addressed to God the Father. Then the *body* of the letter would be directed to any one of the Three Persons, according to their function and the nature of your petition (see 1 Thessalonians 3:11; Acts 7:59; Matthew 9:38). And when you come to the *close* of your letter, obviously you would not sign off in your own name but in the name of our great High Priest (see John 14:13), because His name communicates authority, sacrifice, holiness, perfection, deliverance and forgiveness of sin—none of which we possess in and of ourselves. Therefore, the entire Trinity is involved in our prayers, since they are to be *directed* to the Father, *interpreted* by the Spirit and *validated* by our Lord Jesus Christ.

Jesus planted balance in the soil of this greeting. "Our Father" speaks of immanence, but "in heaven" speaks of transcendence. He is our Father, but He is not to be approached flippantly or irreverently. The one who petitions God must not take Him for granted, for Jesus' greeting is wrapped with not only familial simplicity ("Our Father") but with regal sovereignty ("in heaven").

"Hallowed Be Thy Name . . ." (Verse 9)

Having given us instruction to whom we should pray, the Lord now directs us to associate adoration and praise with the Father's name. This phrase specifically means "Let Your name be revered; let Your name be adored throughout the world; let Your name be treated as holy."

The Greek word for "hallowed" is *hagiazo*, meaning "to set apart, to sanctify, to make holy." How then does His name become hallowed in us? It is by our yielding to His authority, submitting to His will and ascribing all praise, honor and glory to our living God. Since all is *from* Him and *through* Him, all must be *to* Him and *for* Him (see Romans 11:36).[5] Thus, praise, adoration and worship are central in this prayer of petition.

"Thy Kingdom Come . . ." (Verse 10)

Next, our Lord directs us to pray for His kingdom in heaven to be manifested in the hearts of men on earth. This has a direct reference to Messiah's preaching during His earthly ministry that "the kingdom of heaven is near" (Matthew 4:17). As regenerated believers, we must live with the expectancy of His imminent return. Thus, a portion of our prayer should be, "Lord Jesus, come quickly, for being with You I desire nothing on earth." However, as He tarries, we must pray for and be engaged in the multiplication of souls who will acknowledge Him as Savior and Lord—the Ruler of their lives. This requires obedience on our part to the Great Commission, as stated in Matthew 28:19-20.

"Thy Will Be Done as in Heaven So on Earth . . ." (Verse 10)

The Lord instructs us to pray for His will to be fulfilled throughout society and particularly within our lives. I like how one theologian defined prayer and its association with the will of God: "Prayer is not the means by which man gets his will done in heaven, but the means by which God gets His will done on earth."

To see the perfect will of God accomplished in your life demands the total surrender of your mind, emotions and will to His sovereignty. Otherwise, the Enemy, that wicked serpent, will hold sway within your will. Matthew Henry expressed it well: "All the wickedness of the wicked world is owing to the willfulness of the wicked will."[6] Therefore, we must die to self on a daily basis in order for the will of God to be fulfilled within our lives (see Luke 9:23).

"Give Us This Day Our Daily Bread . . ." (Verse 11)

Here is the first and only petition in which we ask God to "give us" something to meet our personal needs. Notice that we are not instructed to ask for annual, monthly or even weekly bread but only for "daily bread." Certainly this would include all our physical needs (though not all our wants); but as mature believers, our greatest concern should be for the nourishing of our souls.

When Jesus incorporated this petition into His model, He gave us not only evidence of our dependence upon God but inserted a window to look at God's willingness to invest in the physical realm of our lives. The Father in heaven is concerned not only with *spiritual formation* but also *physical preservation*. It still pleases Him to hear us access the throne room for the basic needs of life. If the concerns of the kingdom are the priority in our lives, He will certainly take care of our material and physical needs, as affirmed in Matthew 6:33: "But seek first his kingdom and his righteousness, and all these things will be given to you as well." He still supplies "manna and quail."

"And Forgive Us Our Offenses, As We Have Forgiven Our Offenders . . ." (Verse 12)

Most of the petitions in this prayer, in one fashion or another, had been commonly used by the Jews in their devotions. However, this instruction of forgiveness was new to them. Jesus not only introduces it here and in verses 14 and 15, but He reinforces it in His parable of the unmerciful servant in Matthew 18:23-35.

Notice the composition of this petition. There are two transactions: a *vertical* one ("Forgive us our offenses") and a *horizontal* one ("as we have forgiven our offenders"). In order to be pardoned for our sins, the *horizontal* must precede the *vertical* or we curse ourselves when we recite the Lord's Prayer. Remember that if we fail to forgive others, we burn the bridge through which we ourselves must pass. An integral part of our communion with God should be given to asking the Spirit of Truth to examine our hearts for anything contrary to Him. (More attention will be given to this in the chapters on confession with repentance.)

"And Do Not Let Us Enter into Temptation, but Deliver Us from Evil . . ." (Verse 13)

The Lord includes both a positive and a negative side of this petition. The negative directs us to ask the Father *not* to allow us to enter a "place of testing where a solicitation to do evil would tempt us to sin."[7] In other words, we are asking for protection *against* evil. This is followed by the positive side, where we are to ask for deliverance *from* the Evil One. When we pray for the hedge of the Spirit to encircle our lives, families, churches, etc., we are literally praying for protection *against* and deliverance *from* the assaults of the Destructive One himself.

"For Thine Is the Kingdom and the Power and the Glory for Ever and Ever. Amen." (Verse 13)

Jesus concludes the prayer with praise to the Father and an implied declaration that it is only His kingdom that we seek, it is only His power that will manifest His will and it is only His holiness that will be glorified for ever and ever.

This model prayer of petition begins with *adoration* ("Hallowed be Thy name") and closes with *worship* and *praise* ("glory for ever and ever"). And in between the two, you can find many places for *thanksgiving* and *confession with repentance*, all of which will be thoroughly reviewed in the remaining chapters.

Study Questions

Personal Study

1. Read Psalm 66:18. Why does this verse indicate our need to pray for ourselves before we pray for others?
2. Read Matthew 6:9-13. The author says that the Lord's Prayer begins with "Our Father in heaven" to show God's immanence (closeness) and also His transcendence (majestic glory). Spend some time meditating on how a proper and complete picture of God's attributes affects how we pray.
3. What does it mean to pray, "Thy kingdom come"? What can we do to help usher in His kingdom (see Matthew 28:19-20)?
4. Read Luke 9:23. How does this Scripture relate to the prayer "Thy will be done as in heaven so on earth"?
5. Compare Matthew 6:11 to 6:33. How do these two verses relate to each other? What does this teach you about your own prayer life?
6. Review the pattern of verses 12 and 13 as mentioned in the last two pages of the chapter: Forgiving others leads to receiving forgiveness; being guided away from temptation and delivered from evil leads to praise and worship. How has this pattern repeated itself in your life?

Group Study

1. As a group, come up with a definition of the word *petition*. How close is it to the author's definition on page 98?

2. Have someone read Matthew 6:9-13. What does the author say is the definition of the word *hallowed*? How does God's name become hallowed in us? Discuss.

3. Return to the definition of *petition* that the group agreed upon in the first question. Discuss how this relates to the prayer "Thy will be done." How do our needs and wants fit into God's will?

4. How does the group's definition of *petition* fit in with the prayer "Give us this day our daily bread"?

5. Is it fair for God to link His forgiveness of us with our forgiveness of others? Read Matthew 18:23-35 and discuss.

6. As a group, go through Matthew 6:9-13 and identify as many elements of prayer as you can. (You should be able to find such elements as adoration, worship, praise, petition and confession.)

7. Close in prayer, asking God to show you how to follow the pattern of the Lord's Prayer in your own prayer closet.

7
Praise, Adoration and Worship

Whom or what we worship invariably determines the course and outcome of our lives (see Psalm 115:3-8). *How* we worship reflects our understanding of and attitude toward the attributes of our God. This is why the psalmist writes, "Blessed [spiritually prosperous] are those who have learned to acclaim you" (89:15). The word translated *acclaim* means to praise, to joyfully lift one's voice to God. This verse implies that praise, adoration and worship are a learning process; we come to joyfully applaud our triune God, and in learning to praise Him properly, we have the grand promise of spiritual prosperity.

Three of the most essential elements of a prayer life that leads to intimacy with God are the acts of praise, adoration and worship. *Praise is the acknowledgment of an adoring heart that worships the Giver of all blessings of life. Adoration is reverence and utmost respect for the holiness of God. And worship is an acknowledgment of the personal worth of God.*

The personal worth of God can be found by focusing upon who He is (His attributes) and what He has done (His deeds). The book of Psalms is the ideal prayer book for the proper worship of God; it is replete with His attributes and mighty acts.

The Blessings of Praise, Adoration and Worship

Those who practice praise not only give glory to God but become the recipients of multitudes of blessings beyond comprehension. The former archbishop of Canterbury, William Temple, gave a profound definition of worship by enumerating the benefits (bold) of focusing upon the attributes (italicized) of God:

> To worship is:
> **to quicken the conscience** by the *holiness* of God,
> **to feed the mind** with the *truth* of God,
> **to purge the imagination** by the *beauty* of God,
> **to open the heart** to the *love* of God, and
> **to devote the will** to the *purpose* of God.[1]

Is your praise of God having these effects on your soul, whether you praise Him in your secret closet or in the company of believers? If not, then in all probability you are not engaged in true worship of God but focusing upon something far less than His majestic attributes and mighty deeds. True worship is always God-centered, not man-centered.

Let's look at a few specific blessings that flow from this indispensable element of prayer.

Praise Nourishes the Soul

"I will praise you as long as I live," vows David. "My soul will be satisfied as with the richest of foods; / with singing lips my mouth will praise you" (Psalm 63:4-5).

From this declaration, it appears that praise is like fresh manna ("soul food") from heaven, for as we seek Him, He in turn feeds us "with the richest of foods," meaning that he causes our hearts to rejoice, to sing and to be revived. David also declares, "From you comes the theme of my praise. / . . . They who seek the LORD will praise Him— / may your hearts live forever!" (22:25-26). He reveals the source of all praise ("from you") and then implies that a quickened and revived heart will be the lot of those who seek Him through praise.

Praise is an earthly transaction that carries with it a heavenly explanation. I can't quite comprehend it. However, I do know that when my soul is downcast and my heart is discouraged, I find the cure through praising God, for as I focus on His attributes, it invariably produces a revived and rejoicing heart. Apparently, the Sons of Korah knew this truth, for in the midst of their discouragement, they cried out in Psalm 85:6, "Will you not *revive* us again, / that your people may *rejoice* in you?"

Personal revival is initiated at this very point. When you focus on the attributes of the Almighty and sincerely acknowledge who He is, He then sends "times of refreshing" into the depths of your soul—all by the quickening power of our Comforter, the blessed Holy Spirit.

Praise Prepares the Heart to Become Pure

As you enter into your secret closet and focus upon the holiness, majesty and justice of the Almighty, your heart becomes sensitive to sin. Isaiah certainly experienced this truth when he entered into God's presence:

"Woe to me! . . . I am ruined! For I am a man of unclean lips, and I live among a people of unclean lips, and my eyes have seen the King" (Isaiah 6:5). Even the best of His saints have reason to be ashamed when they enter into the presence of God, for His holiness will always reveal their unholiness.

To hasten this process of purifying the heart, we are exhorted in Psalm 100:4 to "enter his gates with thanksgiving / and his courts with praise; / give thanks to him and praise his name." It serves us well to begin our times of prayer with praise, for when we lift our eyes to the Lord and focus on His perfection, we become abundantly aware of our imperfections. It's as though the Master takes a plow to the turf of our souls and begins a gracious work of "break[ing] up [the] unplowed ground" (Hosea 10:12).

"Unplowed ground" is composed of those blind spots that hinder our relationship with Him and others—it is nothing less than unconfessed sin. And as we confess, repent and appropriate the fullness of the Holy Spirit, our innermost beings begin to celebrate, for we have been cleansed, refreshed and revived.

Praise Offers Something Precious to God

God loves to hear our sacrifices of praise! Hebrews 13:15 affirms this in the form of a command: "Through Jesus . . . let us continually offer to God a sacrifice of praise—the fruit of lips that confess his name." The word *sacrifice* in this context means *"offering something precious to God."* Since Jehovah offered His Son as the great sacrifice of atonement, He desires from us a sacrifice of acknowledgment through the continuous praise of His holy name. When we do this in all our circumstances of life—good and bad—He is pleased and faith-fully responds by bestowing favor upon His children.

David certainly understood this truth, for he offers up a sacrifice of praise in advance of his deliverance from his adversaries in Psalm 54:6: "I will sacrifice a freewill offering to you; / I will praise your name, O LORD, / for it is good." With his confidence mounting as he prays, he begins to see his future as though it were the past, for he states in verse 7, "For he has de-livered me from all my troubles."

Several years ago I was privileged to meet a living translation of this truth through the life of a very pre-cious saint. Miss Bender was a dear friend of my mother and a fellow resident in a nursing home. A retired mis-sionary who had faithfully served the Lord for over forty years in Africa, Miss Bender was now in her late eighties and confined to a wheelchair. She could not have weighed more than seventy-five pounds soaking wet.

I'll never forget our first meeting. After a few prelim-inary pleasantries, she made a most surprising state-ment: "Oh, how I praise God for being in this nursing home." I had *never* heard of anyone praising God for being in such a place, so I asked her if she *really* meant that. With her beady eyes looking over the spectacles perched on the end of her nose, she responded in her high-pitched voice with an emphatic "Yes!" followed by a lengthy discourse on how God had demonstrated His favor by placing her in this nursing home.

In the midst of our discussion, she compared the nursing home with the "holding patterns" that air traf-fic controllers use in directing aircraft during inclem-ent weather. By now I thought this poor soul had really "lost it," so I asked her to explain.

"Well," she responded, "when the weather gets bad at the airports, those men in the tower instruct the pilots to circle at their assigned altitudes and wait until the weather clears before they are permitted to land at their destinations. Likewise, this nursing home is a holding pattern. We're all waiting to go to our destinations—either heaven or hell—and praise God, He's put me in the middle of all this traffic!"

Indeed He had, for Miss Bender had led thirty-one ladies to Christ—out of eighty-one residents in the home! In addition, she was discipling those women every Tuesday evening. On one occasion she invited me to teach them on the power of prayer. I demurred, suggesting that I would sit at her feet along with her elderly students. On that particular evening her theme was centered around a most timely question: "What should we old saints be doing as we wait for the imminent return of Christ, or our homegoing, whichever occurs first?" She then proceeded to give a short sermon on each of her five points:

1. We must read our Bibles.
2. We must pray.
3. We must love one another.
4. We must not fail to assemble.
5. We must sing to the Lord.

When she got to the last point, with her high, squeaky and shrill voice, she strung out the word *sing* for about five seconds. Then she proceeded to give instruction on Ephesians 5:19 by encouraging her sisters on how to effectively praise and worship God.

I will always cherish that evening and the many other occasions I shared with that grand old saint. Not only did she have a grasp of the Scriptures intellectually, but, oh, how she lived it *experientially*! Here was a woman who had given the best years of her life to the service of her King in a distant land, only to end up with a crippled and decrepit body in a nursing home. She could have become a very angry and bitter person, but by the grace and mercy of God, she had learned the practice of offering something precious to the Lord—a sacrifice of praise. And for His part, the Good Shepherd not only provided for all her needs but even extended her missionary call in the winter years of her life to the Overlook Nursing Home in New Wilmington, Pennsylvania.

Praise Liberates the Soul

In Psalm 142:7 we find David hiding from King Saul. He cries out, "Set me free from my prison, / that I may praise your name." Tragically, many Christians are held in bondage because they have never learned to become agents of praise. Their symptoms are most conspicuous: a refusal to engage in public worship, a lack of praise in private devotions and an absence of joy and gladness of heart. These flaws reveal their desperate need for liberation and revival, for they have "hit bottom" spiritually, whether they realize it or not.

What, then, is the cure? Praise and worship! The psalmist declares in Psalm 67:5-7:

> May the peoples praise you, O God;
>   may all the peoples praise you.
> Then the land will yield its harvest,
>   and God, our God, will bless us.
> God will bless us,
>   and all the ends of the earth will fear him.

In this missionary psalm the writer is appealing for the extension of God's grace to the uttermost parts of the earth. And in the midst of his supplication, he expresses the desire that all tongues, tribes and nations might come to participate in the worship of Jehovah: "May all the peoples praise you."

We glean from this instruction the transcendent power of praise and how it "will yield its harvest." What does the writer mean by "harvest"?

Certainly it refers to material and physical prosperity, but the emphasis is on the harvest of spiritual blessings that flow from effectual praise. It implies the favor of God being demonstrated through the reviving of His people, the awakening of the masses, the extension of His kingdom and finally, the ruination of Satan's domain. All of this leads to that glorious day when "all the ends of the earth will fear him."

Hallelujah! Bring it on, Lord!

But notice that it all begins and is sustained through praise. Oh, that we may become the praising saints that He so desperately desires us to be!

Praise Generates Triumphant Faith

One of the most striking illustrations of the victorious power of praise is found in Second Chronicles 20. King Jehoshaphat and the people of Judah are about to be attacked by their enemies. After inquiring of the Lord by declaring a national fast and sacred assembly (see 2 Chronicles 20:3-4), the Lord responds by giving them assurance that this battle is not theirs but His (see 20:15). Furthermore, He gives them the battle plan to march down to the Pass of Ziz where they will find their enemy at the end of the gorge (see 20:16). Once again, He assures them of His presence and deliverance (see 20:17). Then the text informs us:

> Early in the morning . . . [a]fter consulting the people, Jehoshaphat appointed men to sing to the LORD and to praise him for the splendor of his holiness as they went out at the head of the army. (20:20-21)

Certainly, Jehoshaphat and the children of Judah were faced with an enormous "mountain." You may recall from the diagrams in chapter 3 that a mountain is a testing, trial or affliction—*anything* that threatens to prevent you from being and doing all that God wants you to be and do.

In this case, Judah's mountain could have been a lack of faith in God's plan. After all, from a human perspective, it was a ludicrous strategy. But Jehoshaphat demonstrated great faith by not only acting on God's instruction but by appointing a *choir* to lead his army into battle!

Can you imagine General Patton calling on the West Point Glee Club to precede his Third Army as they swept across Europe in World War II? Hardly! But this is precisely what King Jehoshaphat did. In an awesome demonstration of great faith, they marched off singing, praising and thanking the Lord for His enduring love. Now the climax:

> As they began to sing and praise, the LORD set ambushes against the men of Ammon and Moab and Mount Seir who were invading Judah, and they were defeated. (2 Chronicles 20:22)

Here is the principle: There appears to be in this verse an explosion of God's supernatural power as His people stepped out in faith by singing and praising His mighty name. The critical element for effectual prayer is faith, but the key to triumphant faith is praise.

Many years ago I was teaching on this truth in a New England church. Following one of the evening sessions, an elderly woman with an angelic face approached me and affirmed the instruction. However, she raised the question of not being able to identify with the "mountains of life." I explained to her again that "mountains" are trials, testing and afflictions.

Quickly, she interrupted and said, "Oh, Mr. Burr, I know exactly what you mean, but my problem is that I can't seem to remember ever having any!"

I couldn't believe what I had just heard, so I nodded, smiled and wrote it off as an example of someone with a *very* short memory.

Upon returning to the parsonage that evening, I shared this incident with the pastor. As I was attempting to describe who this woman was, he suddenly burst out in laughter and exclaimed, "Oh, that was Mrs. So-and-so. She's constantly singing and praising the Lord. The reason she can't see the mountains is because she's flying over them at 33,000 feet!"

Many of us tend to fly about three inches above sea level, and every little bump in the road tends to plant us at the "crash site." What we need is that inexplicable power of praise to soar over these "mountains of life." Our elderly sister had discovered this years ago. She was flying at high altitude because she had learned to kick in the afterburner of prayer—engaging in the praise, adoration and worship of our wondrous and glorious God!

Study Questions

Personal Study

1. Review the author's definition of praise and worship on the first and second pages of this chapter. Is your praise and worship God-centered or man-centered? Does your praise/worship focus on the attributes of God or on your own personal declarations and/or desires?
2. Meditate on the following verses from the Psalms: 22:25-26; 63:4-5; 85:6. What does praising God do for our spiritual lives? (See William Temple's list of the benefits of praise on the second page of the chapter.)
3. Read Isaiah 6:1-5. What was Isaiah's reaction to his vision of God in all His glory? How does his experience relate to your times of prayer and worship?
4. Read Hebrews 13:15. According to this verse, what is it that makes our praises precious to God? (See the author's comments for the answer to this question.)
5. The author says that many Christians suffer from these symptoms of bondage: refusal to engage in public worship, a lack of praise in private devotions and an absence of joy and gladness of heart. Do any of these characterize your life? What can a Christian do to be set free from such bondage?

6. Read Second Chronicles 20:20-22. What was Jehoshaphat's battle plan? How can you apply that same strategy to the battles in your life?

Group Study

1. Read the definitions of praise, adoration and worship that the author gives at the beginning of this chapter. Keeping in mind the first question under Personal Study, have your experiences in private and public worship been mostly God-centered or man-centered? Discuss.

2. The author says that personal revival is initiated by praise. Do you agree with this statement? Discuss. Invite members of the group to share how learning to praise God has affected their lives, or ask them to offer a testimony of praise to God for something He has done for them recently.

3. What does the author mean by the phrase "unplowed ground" (see Hosea 10:12)? How do we "break up the unplowed ground" in our lives?

4. Have someone read Psalm 54:6 and Hebrews 13:15. Why is our praise considered a sacrifice?

5. Read Psalm 67:5-7. Discuss the results of praise promised by this passage. Are these blessings only physical, or are they spiritual as well?

6. Have the group look over the diagram at the end of chapter 3 and then read the story of Miss Bender on the last two pages of chapter 7. Discuss her experience and how you can imitate her example. Close in prayer, asking that the members of the group may become people of praise.

8
Thanksgiving

The twin sister of praise is thanksgiving. These two elements of prayer look alike, perform alike and come from the same source, which is gratitude. Despite their similarities, however, they are very distinct and have different purposes. Praise *adores* the Giver of all blessings while thanksgiving *enumerates* the blessings of the Giver. One *praises* God for who He is, and the other *thanks* God for what He has done.

An Attitude of Gratitude

"Thanksgiving" can be defined as *the acknowledgment of a grateful heart that remembers the past mercies of God—an attitude of gratitude.* Thanksgiving has its roots in the grace of the Almighty, which is extended to the believer through Jesus Christ and returns to God in the form of gratitude. Thus, Paul says in Second Corinthians 9:15, "Thanks be to God for his indescribable gift!"

In Psalm 50 we find God warning His people of impending judgment because of their insincere and ritualistic sacrifices. He does not rebuke them for their sacrifices per se but reproves them for their contemptuous attitude that implies that God *needs* their worship. James Montgomery Boice puts it succinctly: "To suppose that our worship contributes anything to God or meets a need in God is the height of absurdity."[1] Tragically, the Israelites lost sight of the purpose of true worship: returning to God a portion of what He has already given to us. So the Lord prescribes the following corrective action:

> *Sacrifice thank offerings* to God,
>   fulfill your vows to the Most High,
> and call upon me in the day of trouble;
>   I will deliver you, and you will honor me.
> (Psalm 50:14-15)

Again, we see this word *sacrifice*, which means offering something precious or pleasing to God. The command to "sacrifice thank offerings" refers to that attitude of gratitude that is in response to what God has done for us. For Christians, this grace is expressed in the form of thanksgiving for His divine providence and particularly for the gift of eternal life. *Where there is no remembrance of past mercies and no consideration of present blessings, there will be the certainty of future rebellion.*

Thanksgiving Can Be an Act of Great Faith

When one hurts deeply, when there is scar tissue on the heart, when things appear to be hopeless—is there a cure? Yes! Possibly the most powerful antidote for such conditions is thanksgiving. And when expressed in such circumstances, it is truly an act of great faith and, therefore, a very pleasing sacrifice to God. The

Apostle Paul teaches us in his letters to the churches of
Thessalonica, Ephesus and Philippi the nature of such
thanksgiving:

> Give thanks in all circumstances. (1 Thessalonians
> 5:18)
>
> Always giving thanks to God the Father for every-
> thing . . . (Ephesians 5:20)
>
> In everything, by prayer and petition, with thanks-
> giving, present your requests to God. (Philippians
> 4:6)

Notice the emphasis that Paul places upon this act
of gratitude: "in everything" and "for everything." The
prepositions *in* and *for* are words that usually express
limitations, but the apostle places no limits on thanksgiving, for we are commanded to give thanks "in everything."

It is normal to give thanks *after* the answer is received, but Philippians 4:6 instructs us to offer thanksgiving as we "present [our] requests to God." This *pre-
answer* gratitude is a preemptive strike against bitterness
and disappointment over *how* and *when* our heavenly
Father chooses to answer. Also, it is an expression of
enormous faith to thank Him in advance of His response. Our understanding that He will always do right
by our petitions prompts us to be grateful to Him before they are answered.

Thanksgiving lifts us above any and all circumstances. If we reach what Sue Monk Kidd calls "the
grateful center,"[2] we will be free from being puppets

to the events of our lives. Richard Foster described this center as "a time and a place where we [are] free of all the grasping and grabbing, all the pushing and shoving, all the disapproving and dissenting."[3] If we live in a context of thanksgiving, our lives will take on a more winsome and holy fragrance. This is the place where Paul is bidding us to establish our permanent residence.

Regardless of your past experiences, present circumstances or future prospects, there is a place for thanksgiving. In the midst of a "Gethsemane" experience, thanksgiving can be extremely difficult, but it demonstrates great faith. It not only reveals your faith in Christ but also reflects upon your understanding of the sovereignty of God.

Since God has the power, authority and willingness to work all things for the good of those who love Him, then in a certain sense He ordains whatever comes to pass (though, of course, He is not the author of sin). This being said, we can better understand the assertions made by Paul in these verses. He is not even remotely suggesting that one thank Satan for evil deeds. On the contrary, we are encouraged to express gratitude to our sovereign God who is in the business of turning perceived tragedies into experiential triumphs.

Thanksgiving Turns a Victim into a Victor!

A few years ago, while teaching on this subject in a local church, I was approached by a professional in his early forties who had just given his life to Christ. He willingly shared his background and the course of events that led up to his regeneration. He mentioned that as a child he had for years been mentally and sexually abused by his mother and was still suffering the consequences of his trauma. Because of this background he was struggling with loving and submitting to a God who would allow this to happen to a child. The very thought of intimate communion with such a God terrorized him.

But my friend learned through the practice of the secret closet to focus on the attributes of God and engage in Scripture praying by specifically applying the various elements of prayer. He came to the realization that God was not a God of violence or treachery but a loving and compassionate Father desiring the best for His children. He came to the point of thanking God for his sufferings by praying through Romans 5:2-4: "And we rejoice in the hope of the glory of God. Not only so, but we also rejoice in our sufferings, because we know that suffering produces perseverance; perseverance, character; and character, hope."

He learned that rejoicing in one's sufferings could only be the result of focusing on God's sovereignty and unfailing love. Therefore, he came to pray, "I thank You, sovereign Lord, by faith, for the sufferings You have allowed me to endure." The Lord had shown him he could rejoice in his sufferings because they provided opportunities to be an overcomer through building perseverance, character and hope. He became a vessel of forgiveness, learning to forgive those who had betrayed him—particularly those who had hurt him the most: his parents. He was now liberated from dragging around that old corpse of the past that had paralyzed his soul for many years. By faith, he could sincerely thank God for the restoration that was taking place in his heart and life.

Today, this brother is flourishing in the Spirit and is being used by God to be an encouragement to others. Thanks be to God that he's a victor and not just another victim![4]

Thanksgiving in the Midst of Loneliness

In the early 1970s my "Proverbs 31" mother came to visit us while our family was living in South Florida. She was a gracious and godly woman who modeled meekness and humility. However, after my father's sudden homegoing in 1963, she had developed various physical ailments and lost the desire to live. I asked a Christian friend who was a physician to give Mother a complete physical examination with the hope of restoring her to a purposeful life.

The exam showed nothing more than a broken heart that had never recovered from the loss of a loved one. There were no physical impairments. And the only remedy that my doctor friend could give was prayer.

That evening my mother and I reviewed the medical reports and the doctor's personal comments. In the midst of our lengthy conversation, I shared with her what I had read in my morning devotions concerning the power of thanksgiving. We opened our Bibles and pondered First Thessalonians 5:18, Ephesians 5:20 and

Philippians 4:6. At the time I was a young believer, only two years into the faith, and my mother was a mature believer in her early seventies.

After much discussion, I asked, "Mother, have you ever come to that point of thanking God, by faith, for taking Dad home and leaving you behind?" She was stunned and shocked by such an absurd question. Her response was, "Son, you have no idea how much I loved your father and how lonely I am. If I could only go 'home' to be with the Lord and Howard, I would be most happy!"

Our dialogue continued for some time by examining those verses: "Give thanks in all circumstances," and "always giving thanks . . . for everything." We talked about those prepositions *in* and *for* and how they covered the whole gamut of life. She admitted that she had known these verses since she was a little girl but had never seen them in this light until now.

We closed out our time that evening by praying together. I'll never forget her prayer. With tears streaming down her face, she prayed, "O Lord, thank You for those thirty-eight wonderful years You gave Howard and me together. I miss him so much. Thank You for illuminating my heart this evening with these truths. Therefore, by faith and out of obedience to Your Word, I thank You for leaving me behind, for certainly You must have a good purpose in all of this. Thank You, my God."

The next morning at breakfast, for the first time in many years, there was a smile and a change in her countenance. After returning to her home in western Pennsylvania, her elderly sister noticed this dramatic change and said, "You must have found a good doctor down there in southern Florida!" Indeed she had, for she had touched the "hem of the garment" of the Great Physician in a way that she had never experienced before.

Yes, there is a time for weeping, mourning and grieving, but there comes that time when one must move out in faith and continue on with the God-given purposes of life. Mother had discovered a power for living that produced blessings never before known in her seventy-two years of life. By her own testimony, the most spiritually prosperous years of her life were the last sixteen, in which she had learned the benefits of thanksgiving. Finally, at the age of eighty-eight, she had her "coronation" when she went home to be with the Lord and, yes, to see Howard again.

What has taken place in your life for which you have not given thanks to God? James, the half-brother of Jesus, certainly must have realized the relationship of joy with suffering and the benefits thereof, for he declared:

> Consider it pure joy, my brothers, whenever you face trials of many kinds, because you know that the testing of your faith develops perseverance. Perseverance must finish its work so that you may be mature and complete, not lacking anything. (James 1:2-4)

Study Questions

Personal Study

1. Read the author's definition of thanksgiving on the first page of the chapter. Are you a grateful person? On a scale of one to ten, with ten be-

ing the highest, rate yourself on how often you show gratitude to God.

2. Ponder this statement: "Where there is no remembrance of the past mercies of God, there will be the certainty of future rebellion." Have you seen this in your life or the lives of others?

3. Read Philippians 4:6 carefully and notice the order in which thanksgiving and prayer are presented. What does this mean for your prayer life?

4. When you read the story of the man who had been sexually abused as a child, did it bring to mind a tragic event in your own life? If so, try following this man's practice of praying through Romans 5:2-4 and ask God to help you rejoice even in your sufferings.

5. The author says that his widowed mother came to a point where she could say to God, "I thank You for leaving me behind, for certainly You must have a good purpose in all of this." Does this bring to mind a situation in your life that doesn't make sense? If so, ask God to help you trust in His good purposes and to be thankful.

6. Follow the advice of the song "Count Your Blessings" and list on paper ten things for which you are, or should be, thankful. Share this list with the Lord in prayer.

Group Study

1. Have the group review the first page of the chapter. What is the distinction that the author makes between praise and thanksgiving? Why are both important to one's Christian life?

2. Discuss this comment by the author: "Where there is no remembrance of past mercies and no consideration of present blessings, there will be the certainty of future rebellion."

3. Have someone read First Thessalonians 5:18 and Ephesians 5:20. What does Paul mean by giving thanks in and for everything? Should we thank God for difficulties and pain? How does faith fit into this? Discuss.

4. How can having a thankful heart and rejoicing in suffering help us to find it in our hearts to forgive others? (See the story of the man who had been sexually abused as a child for help in discussing this question.)

5. Have someone read James 1:2-4 and discuss. How does God build perseverance in us? Where does thankfulness fit into this process?

6. Ask each member of the group to name one thing for which he or she is thankful to God. Then ask, "Is there anything within your life for which you have not thanked God?" Close in prayer.

9
Confession: Searching the Heart

Any discussion of the secret closet brings up a sobering and unpopular subject, one that has been spurned by some, swept aside by others and tolerated by many for the purpose of peace at any cost. It has produced untold calamity down through the ages, even dividing the Church. Each of us has been affected by it. And how we deal with it determines the course of our lives and the effectiveness of the Church at large.

I am speaking, of course, of *sin*.

If it were not for sin, our prayers would consist only of praise, adoration, worship and thanksgiving. There would be no need to deal with the next element of prayer: confession with repentance.

The reality of life, however, is that we do live in a sin-soaked world and have been appointed by our Master to be a brilliant and piercing light in the center of this ever-present darkness. Possibly the greatest challenge for believers living in the twenty-first century is to maintain a pure and unwavering commitment to the Lord Jesus Christ in the midst of a culture that has lost its moral compass. I'm mindful of what the late Charles H. Malik shared with me in the early '80s:

> Without Jesus Christ being rediscovered and being relived in the hearts of men in this corrupt world,

the moral decay that we see all around us is going to do us all in. By "corruption" and "moral decay" I mean: (1) the dissolution of the family, the fact that about every other person is either divorced or planning to divorce; (2) the frightful spread of pornography in books, magazines and the cinema; (3) the so-called "sexual revolution"; (4) what is being taught and practiced about morals in the greatest universities; (5) the total absence of the transcendent; (6) the fact that although wisdom begins with the fear of God there is precious little of that fear in the world today; (7) the worship of matter and means and the absence of the great uplifting themes of the spirit; and (8) the will to power everywhere and in everything.

And despite all of these afflictions, people still talk self-deludingly about a spiritual revival. I wish a hundred million people in the United States and the West in general would put on sackcloth and ashes for forty days, weeping and repenting. People do not weep these days, and who repents? And how can we repent of our innumerable sins without weeping? The power of self-delusion is today perhaps the greatest enemy of Jesus Christ.[1]

Tragically, the above characteristics are all too pervasive across our land and have led to impotency in some quarters of the Church. Instead of our light piercing the darkness, the patterns of the world are permeating the hearts of God's people. And I am convinced that these grievous conditions can be traced to four specific areas: (1) the erosion of the fear and wonder of God, (2) the failure to see sin as God sees it—the "downsizing" of His Word, (3) superficial communion with the living God and (4) the absence of authentic confession with repentance.

What then is the corrective action? Since the core issue is sin, we must search it out, examine its consequences and then allow the Great Physician to remove it. If left unattended, sin will grow easily and become more frequent and even habitual. In the process, the guilty one becomes unteachable, obstinate, unrepentant and finally a hindrance to the extension of Christ's kingdom on earth.

An Overview of Sin

The word *sin* literally means "to miss the mark" of God's will and perfection. It is anything contrary to the character of God. It is selfishness and rebellion against the Creator. For thirty-eight years my heart was consumed with this deadly disease and in desperate need of healing and forgiveness from my Maker. Finally, after hearing the "cure" presented by Dr. Bill Bright, I responded by repenting and placing my faith in Jesus as Savior and Lord. I experienced His gracious forgiveness of my sin—past, present and future.

However, after this second birth, I discovered that I was not perfect, that I still had a tendency to do things "my way." I found myself struggling with pride, arrogance, thinking the worst of others instead of the best. Again, I was in need of forgiveness—*not forgiveness that leads to salvation (that had been dealt with at conversion), but forgiveness of the sins that kept me from fellowship with God.*[2]

This distinction is essential if we are to maintain intimacy with God and fellowship with other believers. If these sins are not confessed, they break our fellowship with the Lord. *Unconfessed sins are sins that we are aware of but because of stubbornness, ego and coldness of heart, we refuse to acknowledge and confess them before God and repent.* If we profess to be believers and fail to acknowledge and confess our sins, then "we make him out to be a liar and his word has no place in our lives" (1 John 1:10).

Furthermore, we have the mandate from the Lord Jesus to keep our hearts cleansed. When dealing with the hypocrisy of the Pharisees and teachers of the law, He exhorted:

> Woe to you . . . you hypocrites! You clean the outside of the cup and dish, but inside they are full of greed and self-indulgence. Blind Pharisee! *First clean the inside of the cup and dish, and then the outside also will be clean.*
> . . . You hypocrites! You are like whitewashed tombs, which look beautiful on the outside but on the inside are full of dead men's bones and everything unclean. In the same way, on the outside you appear to people as righteous but on the inside you are full of hypocrisy and wickedness. (Matthew 23:25-28)

How foolish to wash the *outside* of a cup, which is seen by others, only to leave the *inside*—which is the part you use—dirty! So it is with those who are consumed with *outer* appearances to impress others, only to leave their hearts corrupt—which is repugnant to God. The solution is to cleanse ourselves from the *inside out*: "For from within, out of men's hearts, come evil thoughts, sexual immorality, theft, murder, adultery, greed, malice, deceit, lewdness, envy, slander, arrogance and folly. All these evils come from inside and make a man 'unclean' " (Mark 7:21-23).

We need time in the secret closet to allow the Spirit of truth to search our hearts for anything that is hindering our relationship with the triune God. As the Apostle Paul suggested, "Since we have these promises, dear friends, let us purify ourselves from everything that contaminates body and spirit, perfecting holiness out of reverence for God" (2 Corinthians 7:1).

Ransacking the Heart

As we suggested in our study of praise, adoration and worship, one of the benefits of praise is that it prepares the heart to become pure. When we focus upon the attributes of God, there is always a quickening of soul. For example, in Psalm 139 David is meditating upon the wonders of God's omniscience, omnipresence and omnipotence; in return, the Spirit of God directs him to cry out: "Search me, O God, and know my heart: try me, and know my thoughts: And see if there be any wicked way in me, and lead me in the way everlasting" (139:23-24, KJV).

In essence David was asking God to ransack his heart, to conduct a thorough search for anything that would hinder him from living an upright life. Likewise, we must include times of introspection in our daily devotions for the purpose of maintaining pure hearts.

But keep in mind that this searching of heart is exclusively the work of the Holy Spirit. J. Edwin Orr taught, "It is to the Holy Spirit that the Christian must look if he is to find a measure of revival for his searching soul. Spiritual blessing for believers is dependent on a *cleansing*, which in turn depends upon *confession* that is dependent on *conviction*; and conviction comes from a *searching of heart* by God's own Spirit."[3]

Therefore, each of us needs to get alone with God regularly and allow Him to search our hearts, to plumb the deepest crevices of our souls for anything contrary to His character. In addition to using the Word, a great aid for facilitating this process is the popular prayer-hymn written by Orr in 1936 during the New Zealand revival. He was so caught up in the Spirit that while waiting in line at a local post office, he penned the following lyrics in just eighteen minutes:

> Search me, O God, and know my heart today,
>   Try me, O Savior, know my thoughts, I pray.
> See if there be some wicked way in me;
>   Cleanse me from every sin and set me free.
>
> I praise Thee, Lord, for cleansing me from sin;
>   Fulfill Thy Word and make me pure within.
> Fill me with fire where once I burned with shame,
>   Grant my desire to magnify Thy name.
>
> Lord, take my life and make it wholly Thine;
>   Fill my poor heart with Thy great love divine.
> Take all my will, my passion, self and pride;
>   I now surrender, Lord, in me abide.
>
> O Holy Ghost, revival comes from Thee;
>   Send a revival—start the work in me.
> Thy Word declares Thou wilt supply our need;
>   For blessings now, O Lord, I humbly plead.[4]

This Spirit-inspired hymn gives the essentials for getting right with God—searching, convicting, confessing, cleansing and surrendering—all of which precede revival. Notice how he closes by stating his need for personal revival: "Start the work in me." This should be the cry of every Christian!

Consequences of Unconfessed Sin

This searching of the heart is indispensable for weeding out the impurities of body and soul. If we fail to do it, we can expect the consequences of unconfessed sin.

1. It Breaks Our Fellowship with God

The Israelites were a fickle and disorderly bunch. While praying and fasting for deliverance from their afflictions, they accused God of insensitivity to their plight (see Isaiah 58:3). They failed to remember that neither length of time nor strength of enemies will ever shrink the power of God.

The prophet Isaiah found it necessary to correct them. "Surely the arm of the LORD is not too short to save, / nor his ear too dull to hear" (59:1). In other words, God doesn't have a crippled arm or impaired hearing. On the contrary, the problem was with the Israelites. "But your iniquities have separated / you from your God; / your sins have hidden his face from you, / so that he will not hear" (59:2).

Unconfessed sin will always short-circuit our communion with the Almighty. The psalmist, when testifying to God's favor upon his life, was very much aware of this truth when he declared, "If I had cherished sin in my heart, / the Lord would not have listened" (Psalm 66:18). If we have favorable thoughts of sin, fantasizing in it, treating it as a welcome guest, rolling it under the tongue as a delectable morsel, how can we expect God to listen to our prayers? The corrective action? Confess and repent!

2. It Contaminates the Soul

The prophet Haggai, when challenging the people of Judah to give careful thought to their spiritual lethargy, asked their leaders two thought-provoking questions:

> "If a person carries consecrated meat in the fold of his garment, and that fold touches some bread or stew, some wine, oil or other food, does it become consecrated?"
> The priests answered, "No."
> Then Haggai said, "If a person defiled by contact with a dead body touches one of these things, does it become defiled?"
> "Yes," the priests replied, "it becomes defiled."
> (Haggai 2:12-13)

These two questions deal with ceremonial matters of the Law with which the priests were very familiar. The first question specifically deals with the transmission of holiness, to which they answer "No"—holiness *cannot* be transferred. The second question deals with the transmission of sin, and their response is "Yes"—sin (defilement) *can* be transferred.

The principle here is this: *Just as good health is not contagious but bad health is, so holiness is not transferable but sin is.* Sin is contagious and contaminating. If you leave a rotten apple in a barrel of apples, it will only be a matter of time until the whole batch is rotten. This same truth applies to sin, and for this reason God hates it. Sin not only defiles the heart of the sinner who rebels against God, but if left unattended it can contaminate a whole congregation. The worst scenario that a local congregation could ever experience would be to force the hand of God to place a quarantine sign over its front door: "DO NOT ENTER—THIS CHURCH IS CONTAMINATED"—all because of this infectious disease of sin!

The Apostle Paul certainly realized this contaminating effect of sin, for he challenged the church at Corinth to separate themselves from the sinning brother by warning them, "Don't you know that a little yeast [sin] works through the whole batch of dough? Get rid of the old yeast that you may be a new batch without yeast" (1 Corinthians 5:6-7).

The corrective action? Confess and repent!

3. It May Cause Sickness or Death

Another consequence of unconfessed sin may be sickness of body, though sickness and death are not always a result of sin. This is clearly illustrated in Psalm 38, where David, a man after God's own heart, is consumed with sickness and thus becomes sensitive to his sin:

> O LORD, do not rebuke me in your anger
>   or discipline me in your wrath.
> For your arrows have pierced me,
>   and your hand has come down upon me.
> Because of your wrath there is no health in
>   my body;
>   my bones have no soundness because of my sin.
> My guilt has overwhelmed me
>   like a burden too heavy to bear.
>   (38:1-4)

God is holy, and He will not tolerate unconfessed sin within the hearts of His children, even among His choicest of servants. He is slow to anger and quick to love, but we dare not force His loving sword to pierce our hearts in order to get our attention. If we refuse to deal with our sin, we can expect His chastisements to overcome us in order that He may faithfully deal with our rebellion.

The Apostle Paul confirms that sin can cause sickness and even suggests that it can lead to death. After rebuking the believers at Corinth for their carnal behavior and irreverent attitudes while partaking of the Lord's Supper, he adds, "That is why many among you are weak and sick, and a number of you have fallen asleep [i.e., died]" (1 Corinthians 11:30).

What then should we do? We desperately need to enter the secret closet of prayer and ask God to search and probe our hearts for anything that may be displeasing to Him. To do otherwise is folly. I suggest that we pray something like this:

> *Lord, I ask that You search my heart to see if there be any wicked way in me, any corrupt inclination, any impure thoughts; reveal it, root it out and make me right with You. My desire is to be more Christlike and to pursue Your righteous ways for all eternity.*

We must daily take the time to get alone with God and to allow the convicting power of the Holy Spirit to search our hearts. And as He reveals the sin, our responsibility is to confess it and repent of it.

Study Questions

Personal Study

1. The author says that unconfessed sin results in self-delusion. If we are self-deluded, is there any hope? What things can reveal our sin to us?

2. Read and meditate on Psalm 139:23-24. Put this prayer of David in your own words and offer it up to God as the prayer of your heart. (See the last page of the chapter for the author's own wording of this prayer.)

3. Why is it important to let the Holy Spirit search our hearts before we begin praying for our needs (see Psalm 66:18)?

4. Read First Corinthians 5:6-7. Paul is saying that a whole church can be affected if one member is harboring unconfessed sin. What does Paul say that the church should do? If the person confesses and repents, what should the church do (see 2 Corinthians 2:5-8)?

5. Read Psalm 38:1-4. What is causing David's sickness? What do you think will cure him? What does this say about God's attitude toward unconfessed sin?

6. Meditate on the fourth affirmation in the Prayer Covenant (see appendix A). Pray for the Lord to help you be faithful to this affirmation.

Group Study

1. Read the definition of unconfessed sin on page 134. If we continue to leave sin unconfessed, what does it do to our relationship with God (see 1 John 1:10)?

2. The author says, "We need time in the secret closet to allow the Spirit of truth to search our hearts for anything that is hindering our relationship with the triune God." Discuss this statement. How does this searching of the heart happen? Invite members of the group who have had such an experience to share.

3. Have someone read Isaiah 58:3 and 59:1-2. How does our unconfessed sin change our attitude toward God? How does it change God's attitude toward us?

4. According to Haggai 2:12-13, holiness is not transferable, but sin is. The author compares this to health and sickness: Good health is not contagious, but sickness often is. Can a Christian live in the world and still avoid being contaminated by sin? What is the remedy for this problem? Discuss.

5. Have someone read Psalm 38:1-4 and First Corinthians 11:30. Discuss the concept of God allowing sickness or even death because of unconfessed sin. Does God always work this way? What is His purpose in this?

6. Close by reading together the fourth affirmation in the Prayer Covenant (see appendix A) and praying together for the Lord to help you live a life of repentance and personal revival.

10
Repentance: Healing the Heart

In researching the great spiritual awakenings of the past, J. Edwin Orr discovered five distinguishing characteristics common to all revivals, whether personal or corporate:

1. A spirit of extraordinary prayer
2. Intense conviction of the Holy Spirit
3. Confession of sins with repentance
4. Reconciliation and/or restitution
5. A burden to reach the lost, both near and far[1]

Notice the sequence of these marks of revival. First, there is extraordinary prayer, indicative of hungry and desperate hearts that thirst after fellowship with God. In response, the Mighty One extends His grace through the Holy Spirit by sending intense conviction on the heart. This convicting power of the Spirit is like an irresistible force descending on the soul and creating utter helplessness within.

This was graphically illustrated in the response to the Apostle Peter's divinely inspired sermon following Pentecost. Notice what happens: "When the people heard this, they were cut to the heart and said to Peter and the other apostles, 'Brothers, what shall we do?'" (Acts 2:37).

The phrase "cut to the heart" refers to the irresistible force of the Holy Spirit, creating such utter helplessness within that they cried out, "What shall we do?" It is this convicting power that led them to confess and repent of their sins.

Personal revival pivots on our confession with repentance. There has never been a revival recorded in Church history that did not include confession of sins along with the fruit of repentance.

A Work of Grace

Confession of sin is the result of God's grace working in the heart. Were it not for His grace, all of us would still be immersed in our deadly sins and left hopeless for all eternity. But in His unfailing love He sent His beloved Son not only to rescue us from hell but also to keep us pure and secure through His abounding grace.

Confession is the outward expression of the Holy Spirit's inward conviction.[2] The original Greek word literally means "to say the same thing"; in other words, it means to specifically agree with the Holy Spirit that you are guilty of His accusations. *And the purpose of confession is always to bring healing of the heart by reconciling us with God and with others.* For this reason the Enemy of our souls wars against this element of prayer and will do everything possible to dissuade us from acknowledging and confessing our sins.

As children of God, we should welcome such a work of grace and respond quickly to His merciful promise as given by the Apostle John in his first epistle: "If we confess our sins, he is faithful and just and will forgive us our sins and purify us from all unrighteousness" (1 John 1:9).

Notice the uniqueness of Christ's love being exhibited in this glorious promise to the Church. First, it is conditional as indicated by the use of the preposition *if*. It is not automatic but is only operative as we acknowledge and confess our specific sins to Him.

Next, as we confess our sins to God, we have the absolute assurance of His forgiveness, not because of our confession but because of the cleansing blood that was shed at Calvary—the finished work of Christ on the cross. Not only does He remove the guilt of our sin by His pardoning mercy, but He also purifies us to make us acceptable worshipers and useful servants for our most holy God. By placing our faith, hope and trust in Christ Jesus we can be assured that "he does not treat us as our sins deserve / or repay us according to our iniquities. / For as high as the heavens are above the earth, / so great is his love for those who fear him; / as far as the east is from the west, / so far has he removed our transgressions from us" (Psalm 103:10-12).

Our forgiveness is based solely upon the vicarious sacrifice of Jesus Christ, who not only purchased our salvation but continues to cleanse us and maintain a relationship with us. As Edwin Orr put it:

> The ground of forgiveness is the Cross,
> The price of forgiveness is nothing,
> The condition of forgiveness is confession,
>   and
> The object of forgiveness is maintenance of
>   fellowship with Him.[3]

The Fruit of Repentance

Along with our confession there must be the fruit of repentance—otherwise we will continue to repeat our sins and hinder our intimacy with God. No Christian has ever enjoyed full fellowship with God when he or she has refused to repent of sin. As I mentioned before, if unconfessed sin is left unchecked, it not only pollutes your own soul but has the potential to contaminate your family and local assembly.

Perhaps the most complete definition of repentance would be *to feel such regret ("godly sorrow") over one's sin as to bring about a revolutionary change of mind, leading to a radical change of attitude and behavior.* Repentance puts teeth to our confession to make it genuine and not mere lip service. Orr referred to repentance as "the first word of the gospel," not only for salvation (see Matthew 3:2; 4:17; Acts 2:38) but for the believer's continuing fellowship with Christ (see Revelation 2:5, 16, 22; 3:3, 19).[4] Martin Luther wrote, "When our Lord and Master Jesus Christ said 'repent,' He willed that the entire life of a believer be one of repentance."

Repentance is *not* penitence, and it is a master stroke of Satan to confuse the two. *Penitence* comes from a Latin word meaning sorrow or grief, but *repentance* comes from the Greek word meaning "a change of mind." There is a vast difference between these two words; a person could feel remorse over his or her actions with no change of behavior. But someone who is truly repentant has a change of heart that is demonstrated by a change of attitude and conduct.

Fortunately, repentance is discernible; it bears a fruit that becomes most evident in the life of a mournful sinner. That is why the Apostle Paul, in affirming the Corinthians for their change of heart, could say, "See what this godly sorrow has produced in you: what earnestness, what eagerness to clear yourselves, what indignation, what alarm, what longing, what concern, what readiness to see justice done" (2 Corinthians 7:11).

This is a textbook case of a group of believers who were graciously convicted of their sin and responded in godly sorrow, producing the fruit of authentic repentance: an "earnestness" to please God and ferret out evil; an "eagerness to clear [them]selves" by admitting their waywardness and not attempting to rationalize their sinful behavior; a righteous "indignation" and "alarm" against sin and the tempter; a "longing" and "concern" to reform what went amiss and to make it right; and a "readiness" to accept whatever the consequences may be in order to satisfy the harm done to others. This speaks of a humble, contrite and teachable spirit (see Isaiah 66:2).

This fruit of repentance—where admission of sin is followed by a reversal of action—is the surest sign that God is at work in a person's life. Anything less is remorse, which is the human reaction of disgust at oneself for getting caught.

The Healing of Relationships

The cure for broken fellowship with God and fellow believers is found through the confession of one's sins, accompanied by repentance. This truth is attested to in both the Old and New Testaments and confirmed in the great spiritual awakenings of the past.

But in spite of these assurances, there appears to be much neglect, misunderstanding and abuse of this most essential element of prayer. Therefore, it is necessary to revisit the fundamental purpose of confession. We find this outlined in the epistle of James, where the author is exhorting his brethren, "Confess your sins to each other and pray for each other so that you may be healed" (James 5:16). The Greek word used here for "healed" implies a spiritual healing—a healing of heart—even though the same word is used elsewhere for healing from physical maladies.

However, the principle of confessing your sins "to each other" must be practiced with care. *Confession of sin is always intended to heal relationships, never to further damage them by indiscreet revelations.* Accordingly, there must be discretion with confession; timing is of utmost concern. One should always be led by the Spirit and never driven by guilt alone.

This being said, the question arises, "How far should we go with confession?" Certainly, it begins vertically with God, but how far do we carry this horizontally with others? In other words, does one have to go public with the confession of a very personal sin? The answer is found in the maxim "Let the circle of sin determine the circle of confession." Simply stated, *secret (i.e., personal) sin is to be secretly confessed, private (i.e., small group) sin privately confessed and public sin publicly confessed.*[5] We must deal with sin from the inside out—first between ourselves and the Holy One, then with the other offended parties, through reconciliation and/or restitution. This maxim is meant to be a general guideline, with exceptions being made as the Spirit directs. Now let us review briefly these three types of sin and their corresponding confessions.

1. Secret Sin

This type of sin is between God and the individual alone. Since there is no offended party inside the circle of sin, it is not necessary to confess to another person. For example, you may have a thought life that is not honoring to the holiness of God, or possibly you may be thinking the worst of another brother instead of the best. This is between you and God and should be dealt with accordingly.

While I was doing a conference a few years ago, a sister in Christ approached me and asked for my forgiveness. Since I had never met this woman before, I was puzzled by her request and asked why she needed my forgiveness.

"Well," she responded, "I had these negative thoughts about you and was turned off by some things you said, but now I realize I was wrong."

"Sister," I said, "you don't need my forgiveness; this is an issue between you and God. But if it will comfort you, certainly, I will forgive you."

Remember, *confession is always for healing purposes, never to further exacerbate a strained relationship.* Use discretion when you confess personal sins, remembering that it is an issue that you need to confess to God alone.

King David knew the consequences of withholding confession and conversely the blessings that come with the acknowledgment of sin:

When I kept silent [about my sin],
    my bones wasted away
    through my groaning all day long.
For day and night
    your hand was heavy upon me;
my strength was sapped
    as in the heat of summer.
Then I acknowledged my sin to you
    and did not cover up my iniquity.
I said, "I will confess
    my transgressions to the LORD"—
and you forgave
    the guilt of my sin.
    (Psalm 32:3-5)

2. Private Sin

This type of sin is between God, the perpetrator and any other offended parties inside the circle of sin. The biblical instruction for dealing with private sin was given by our Lord Jesus when He exhorted His disciples, "Therefore, if you are offering your gift at the altar and there remember that your brother has something against you, leave your gift there in front of the altar. First go and be reconciled to your brother; then come and offer your gift" (Matthew 5:23-24).

Notice that reconciliation between God's children is more important to the Lord than their sacrifices to Him. But tragically, many churches are filled with broken relationships, all because of failure to obey the Master's command to "first go and be reconciled to your brother."

The process of reconciliation begins with the perpetrator confessing and repenting of his sin before God, followed by asking the victim for forgiveness and making appropriate amends to satisfy the wounded party. If the victim refuses to accept the apology, it may be necessary to make further attempts at reconciliation. If the offended party does not forgive, the perpetrator can be assured that he is clean before God. The Lord will honor his sincere and earnest attempts, even if reconciliation cannot be completed. The penitent sinner cannot be responsible for the actions of the impenitent victim.

3. Public Sin

Public sin involves the Lord, the perpetrator and large numbers of offended people. And it can occur in two ways:

First, it can be a personal or private sin that becomes public knowledge. For example, we all have heard of the TV evangelist who was caught in the act of adultery. But what is frequently overlooked is that his sin began in secret with the lust of his mind (secret sin); it was followed by the act itself (private sin), which later was exposed in the public arena. Since masses were offended by his transgression, it necessitated public confession with the corresponding fruit of repentance. If we fail to deal with our sin secretly or privately, we can be certain that God has a way of exposing it publicly. His Word promises, "You may be sure that your sin will find you out" (Numbers 32:23).

Second, public sin can also occur in the presence of many people, either by commission or omission. For example, a parishioner in a local church business meeting—with over 100 people in attendance—slandered the recently departed pastor by calling him a liar. That was a public sin of *commission*, for many were greatly offended by such an accusation. Unfortunately, the moderator of the meeting compounded the problem by not calling the brother to account, thus being drawn into the circle of sin by a sin of *omission*. He failed to properly discharge his spiritual duties and responsibilities. This left a gaping wound in the fellowship that could have been healed if the perpetrators had publicly repented.

In both cases the corrective action should have been initiated through *personal* confession, with repentance before God, followed by *private* confession to those closely associated with the situation and, finally, a *public* confession to the wounded masses.

The scriptural support that is most frequently used for the confession of public sin is James 5:16: "Therefore confess your sins to each other and pray for each other so that you may be healed. The prayer of a righteous man is powerful and effective."

The *object* of this public confession is the deliverance from faults, "so that you may be healed." The *means* involved is prayer with specific confession—"confess your sins . . . and pray for each other." But the question that becomes problematic is, how much should one confess publicly?

The general rule is to *be discreet—and also to be certain that you are led by the Spirit and not driven by your guilt.* Specifically, you should give just enough detail to acknowledge your sinfulness and solicit the prayers of fellow believers. Too much detail can be used by others to justify their own sin; they may even be tempted to vicariously participate in the sin.

In summary, we should not allow the sun to go down without settling our sin with God, for He is a holy God who becomes an adversary against any form of unconfessed sin. Second, we must be quick to get right with our wounded brethren by making every effort to be reconciled with those whom we have wounded and forgiving those who have wounded us. To do anything less grieves the Spirit, breaks our fellowship with God, strains relationships and causes spiritual prosperity to cease. For we are promised that "he who conceals his sins does not prosper, but whoever confesses and renounces them finds mercy" (Proverbs 28:13).

A Glorious Ending from an Ignoble Beginning

The blessings of confession with repentance are evident in the following testimony from a local church that had been ensnared with besetting sins. As the members went through the process of dealing with the different levels of sin—secret, private and public— they were gloriously healed of their infirmities.

This testimony begins when this particular congregation had very subtly lost its vision over a period of time. It became indifferent and had developed a spirit of pride because of its spacious and debt-free facilities. To some they were viewed as a "country club" for the well-heeled. However, in God's infinite wisdom He sent them a pastor who was a skilled preacher but had the personality of a drill sergeant. It was only a matter of time before conflict developed between the pulpit and the pew. Relationships became strained, gossip was frequent, lines were drawn and eventually they were hopelessly deadlocked in controversy.

In the midst of this, the church chairman, along with a few other godly men, realized their dilemma and proposed a restoration process at the highest level of authority. This was to include times of solitude with the Lord (i.e., secret or personal confession), followed by times of prayer and interaction with all five of these leaders (i.e., private confession). Though the pastor refused to participate, the others pursued what they believed to be God's will. Eventually, this restoration process was expanded to include all the church leaders.

Several weeks later the entire leadership (except for the pastor, who by then had withdrawn from the church) held a weekend retreat at which they asked God to search the deepest parts of their hearts for anything that would hinder His blessings from flowing upon the congregation. Times of prayer with intense conviction of the Spirit were spent in solitude for *personal* confession and in their small groups for *private* confession, while they waited on God to reveal the corporate sins of the church. As the Lord disclosed their sins of commission and omission, they cataloged them, confessed and repented of them. Furthermore, they agreed to set a date at which the entire church would come together to acknowledge their sins and seek forgiveness from God (i.e., *public* confession). This was to be called a "Day of Confession and Forgiveness." In preparation for that day, they encouraged the flock to spend extended times in prayer. Also, letters seeking forgiveness and reconciliation were sent to offended parties who had subsequently left the church.

For the next three weeks the flock frequented their closets of prayer to purify themselves before God (i.e., *personal* confession). Many met with one another and reconciled past differences (i.e., *private* confession). Finally, the "Day of Confession and Forgiveness" arrived on a Sunday in September. It was a most unusual worship service: There was no sermon, only seasons of prayer that included the public acknowledgment of their cataloged sins (i.e., *public* confession) followed by communion around the Lord's Table. After the service they had dinner together in the joy of a new fellowship with God and one another.

The results were astounding! There was now a new love for Christ and one another; joy was restored. A new spiritual vitality was evident, resulting in the spontaneous sharing of the gospel throughout the community. New lambs were added to the flock on a weekly basis, though the church had never been previously trained in personal evangelism. Also, God had graciously prepared the hearts of His people to welcome and disciple these new converts. All of this glorious blessing flowed through a broken group of laymen who, without pastoral leadership, had recognized God's displeasure and repented of their sin.

A few months later, a friend of mine became their new pastor. Upon his arrival, he was overwhelmed by the attitude of the people and the outpouring of the Spirit. "This is like riding a surf board on the waves of revival," he said on numerous occasions. "I just want to stay out of God's way and enjoy the ride!" And this process of God's amazing grace continued. In a period of five years, the congregation had more than doubled in attendance to 1,000, with over 700 professions having been made for Christ in a community of 21,000 people!

As you can see, all the marks of revival were evident in this work of God's grace: *extraordinary prayer, intense conviction of the Spirit, confession with repentance, reconciliation and a burden to reach the lost.* This is what happens when Christians become broken and realize that they are nothing more than a bunch of continuously repenting sinners. Yes, the psalmist was right when he declared:

> If you, O LORD, kept a record of sins,
> O Lord, who could stand?
> But with you there is forgiveness;
> therefore you are feared.
> (Psalm 130:3-4)

Study Questions

Personal Study

1. The author says that confession with repentance is crucial to personal revival. Based on what was taught in the previous chapter, why would you say this is so?
2. The author defines repentance as a revolutionary change of mind leading to radical changes in attitude and behavior. If this is true, would you define repentance as a one-time decision or a lifestyle? Why?

3. Read James 5:16. If you wished to confess a private sin and ask for prayer, to whom would you go? The author suggests that confession must be practiced with discretion, so that it results in healing, not in a further strain on the relationship. Can you think of a fellow believer whom you could trust with your confession?

4. If you have offended someone by your sin but have repented and confessed it to God and the other person, what further responsibility do you have if the other person refuses to forgive?

5. If you felt that you needed to make a public confession of sin, to whom would you speak about it first? How would you go about making the confession?

6. Meditate on the fifth affirmation in the Prayer Covenant (see appendix A). Pray for the Lord to help you be faithful to this affirmation.

Group Study

1. According to the author, "the purpose of confession is to bring healing of the heart by reconciling us with God and with others." How does confession with repentance bring reconciliation? Discuss.

2. What is the difference between repentance and penitence? Are the believers described in Second Corinthians 7:11 experiencing repentance or penitence? Why?

3. Discuss the meaning of the following statement: "Let the circle of sin determine the circle of confession."

4. When a sin becomes public knowledge or is committed publicly, what is the appropriate method of confession?
5. Look over the story of the church in the last few pages of the chapter. How might such a public confession take place in your local fellowship? Discuss.
6. Close by reading together the fifth affirmation in the Prayer Covenant (see appendix A) and praying together for the Lord to help you take up your crosses daily and to offer yourselves as living sacrifices.

11
Hindrances to Prayer

My mind frequently races back to that epochal week-end of October 10, 1970, when the Gentle Shepherd reached into the depths of my needy soul and rescued me from the slimy pits of mud and mire. Mercifully, He planted my feet on the Rock and placed within my breast a song of praise to the God of Abraham, Isaac and Jacob, the Father of Messiah. He graciously gave me the "language of Canaan" and delivered me from my profane and uncouth habits of the past. Innumerable have been the wonders of His grace over the many years since. Were I to tell them all, there would be a shortage of ink to print them. Suffice it to say that He has "pierced my ear" (see Exodus 21:6) to be a servant and has bestowed upon this frail creature of the dust unfathomable blessings.

I share this because in spite of His awesome favor, there are times when my heart drifts and follows the pursuits of Baal (see Numbers 25:3). Then I find myself in a spiritual desert with my soul dry, drained, downcast and discouraged. But then, once again I turn back to the Giver of all grace and gorge myself on the freshness of His Word by lapping up His satisfying drink from the "streams of living water" (John 7:38).

Invariably, I also become disgusted with myself, wondering, *How long will it be till I get it right?*

As I have pondered this process, which has been repeated many a time over the years, I have concluded that the complete cure will never come until He calls me home; only then will there be total and complete deliverance. In the meantime, there is a life of grace to be lived in the service of the King. And if, by His guiding mercy, I can sidestep a few threatening hindrances that always seem to trip up my heart, then the frequency of repetition will be noticeably diminished.

Therefore, I would like to share from my walk of life a couple of hindrances with which most of us struggle. Overcoming these brings much profit to the soul. *It should be noted that a hindrance is any unconfessed sin that, if not dealt with, undermines our communion and intimacy with Christ.* Hindrances must be confessed and repented of quickly in order to reopen our "life-support system" with the triune God and to enjoy His favor.

There are multitudes of hindrances that could be listed, such as lack of faith, absence of unity between spouses and fellow believers, the sin of presumption, impure motives, etc. However, for our study I will focus only on two, since these are the ones that have given me my greatest grief. Furthermore, from these two transgressions flow all other sin.

A Loss of First Love

Several years ago while conducting a prayer conference in eastern Connecticut, I found myself in need of encouragement from the Lord. Even though the conference had been going well, I was still hurting from a previous "Gethsemane" that had left much scar tissue on my heart. So on this particular morning I moved into my secret closet and there experienced one of the most challenging and convicting times I've ever had in prayer.

I was impressed to pray through the first four chapters of Revelation. It was in the second chapter that the convicting power of the Spirit shook my soul. As I was praying through the first three verses of that chapter, it was as though the Master was affirming me by saying, "Yes, Richard, I know of your circumstances and your deeds. You have been faithful, earnest and persevering. And you have not grown weary in the process."

However, when I moved into the next verses my soul shifted from being cheerful to being very sober as I read:

> Yet I hold this against you: You have forsaken your first love. Remember the height from which you have fallen! Repent and do the things you did at first. If you do not repent, I will come to you and remove your lampstand from its place. (Revelation 2:4-5)

My first reaction was that this obviously didn't apply to me, so I would just move on to the next verses. But the Lord had other intentions. Suddenly, I found myself under intense conviction of the Spirit, attempting to explain myself away by defending my cause. I reminded Him of how I had left the business world and was serving Him by living in steadfast faith, how I loved my calling of encouraging believers to become praying saints. I argued about my sacrificial lifestyle of traveling from church to church, exhorting congregations to become "a house of prayer" and so on.

After my lengthy defense, I sensed Him saying, "Yes, Richard, I'm very much aware of all you have said and particularly your love for your calling. In fact, this is the very grievance I hold against you. You love the gift more than the Giver! You love your ministry more than you love Me!"

Stunned by this revelation, I felt completely helpless, as though my heart had been emptied of all strength. But His instruction didn't cease. He continued by warning that if I did not repent and return to that childlike love of my early years in the faith, then reluctantly He would have to remove His favor from my life and work.

It was as though He was saying, "If you so choose, you may continue as you are, but you will be like an *organization* without an *organism*; you may have *activity*, but no *power*; there may be *growth*, but no *vitality*."

I responded to this convicting encounter with much weeping and repenting. And the result was the glorious reviving of my soul, gratitude for His cleansing, thanksgiving for His faithfulness and rejoicing in His resplendent light. In fact, I was so overcome by this remedial judgment that I asked Him, "Lord, never allow my life to outlive my passion for You; otherwise, just call me home."

This turned out to be a most refreshing time in the presence of the Lord—a gentle *blasting* followed by overwhelming *blessing*.

Over the years I have come to learn that if I do not maintain my passion for Christ, then I become very susceptible to selfish ambition, which is just another word for pride. And this invariably occurs when I fail to show up for my "early morning briefing session." When I forfeit my time of solitude with the Master, the embers of my heart grow cool and my "first love" becomes a memory of the past rather than the reality of the present.

What about you? Could it be said by the Lord, "There is a servant who loves Me with all his heart, soul, mind and strength"? If not, may I encourage you to remember, repent and return to your first love, so that you may be consistently enjoying His presence and favor. Remember, the first and greatest command in the entire Word of God is "Love the Lord your God with all your heart and with all your soul and with all your mind" (Matthew 22:37).

Pride

Arrogance, spiritual elitism, self-righteousness, self-sufficiency, self-gratification—whatever you want to call it, they all have their roots in the mother of all sins: pride. Throughout the ages this sin has brought low the highest and noblest of men and has been the "chief cause of misery for every nation and every family since the world began."[1] There has never been a person on earth who has not struggled with it or been affected by it. Even righteous Job, "the greatest man among all the people of the East" (Job 1:3), fell under its influence. Scripture tells us, "So these three men stopped answering Job, because he was righteous in his own eyes" (32:1).

Unfortunately, Job did not listen to the instruction of Elihu, the young man with the right message. So, the Lord came upon Job like a tornado and eventually got his attention by blitzing him with ninety-one questions (see Job 38-41). Finally, the faithful servant acknowledged his sin, repented, was gloriously restored to fellowship with God and became the recipient of His abounding favor (see Job 42).

I believe that when there is an erosion of our focus on the Almighty, a decay of our "first love" for Christ, it is only a matter of time until our hearts become consumed with the concerns of self. And this overemphasis on self is a fruit of pride. Simply stated, pride is "structuring your world in such a way that it always plays to your benefit, comfort and security."[2] And as believers, we have the audacity to turn around and ask God to bless it.

I found this to be true by personal experience. Back in the mid-1970s, I was asked to lead the "I Found It" evangelistic campaign in New York City. It was an enormous undertaking, and as a relatively young believer I found myself in the midst of much confusion and turmoil. So I asked my friend Bill Kanaga,[3] chairman of our executive committee, to have dinner with me and discuss my plight. He graciously accepted, and we met in a beautiful restaurant atop the Pan-American Building in midtown Manhattan.

During the course of our meal, I shared with him my concerns, never expecting the type of response that I was about to receive. After finishing my lengthy discourse, Bill paused, reflected for a moment and then asked, "I assume you have come to get my advice, so do you mind if I make some observations and ask you a few questions?"

I assured him that this was my purpose in calling him.

Without a further word, he said to me, "Burr, you reek with pride!"

Very unexpectedly, what I thought was going to be an enjoyable and affirming evening turned ugly. I sensed my blood pressure rising as beads of perspiration formed across my brow, and I felt my cheeks burning. The delectable piece of beef that I had previously ingested, which was now headed south in my digestive track, seemed to want to reverse its course and turn north. It would be an understatement to say that I was most uncomfortable.

Bill obviously noticed my reaction, for he smiled and said, "You're angry, aren't you?"

I responded, "Who, me? No, no, no—this is why I'm here, Bill. I need your counsel." I was lying profusely as I attempted to conceal my anger, for deep in my heart I wanted to blast him!

He then continued by asking several questions. I do not recall the nature of his inquiries, but I do remember his response to every one of my answers: "I'm not surprised by your answer, for you reek with pride."

By this time I was so angry and my mind so convoluted that I couldn't even think straight. Mercifully, after about twenty minutes of this inquisition, he finished his questioning and silence fell over our table. Then he motioned to the waiter to give us our check, which he paid. Up to that point, this act of benevolence seemed to be the only positive thing that had occurred.

It was around 10 p.m. when we left the restaurant and headed up Park Avenue. Not a word was spoken. When we arrived in front of his office building, Bill turned and embraced me, saying with deep humility, "Brother, I want you to know that I love you and the only reason I said what I did is that I have just finished working through the same issue myself."

It was a somewhat comforting thought to know that I was in such good company and not the only one who ever struggled with such sin. After a few more cordial exchanges he excused himself to tidy up some unfinished work in his office, and I somberly continued up Park Avenue to my apartment.

Upon retiring that evening, I picked up and started to read the book *Mere Christianity* by C.S. Lewis, which had been given to me several months prior to this occasion. As I was thumbing through it, I noticed that it had been purposely marked at chapter 8 with a paper clip. It was titled "The Great Sin," so I began reading, wondering what this great sin was. My query was soon answered with the following statement in the very first paragraph:

> There is no fault which makes a man more unpopular, and no fault which we are more unconscious of in ourselves than pride. And the more we have it ourselves, the more we dislike it in others.[4]

I thought, *Now isn't this a coincidence—this is precisely what Kanaga was saying tonight!* But this was no accident. It was a divine appointment with the God of all wisdom. Over the next several hours, while under conviction of the Holy Spirit, I cross-referenced Lewis' insights with Scripture, made copious notes and did much repenting. I had come to a new appreciation of Daniel 4:37, as it is strikingly paraphrased in the Living Bible: "For he is able to take those who walk proudly and push them into the dust!"

Lewis mentioned several other characterizations of this most vile sin of which I will only share a few, along with some personal observations.

Pride Is the Total Anti-God State of Mind[5]

All sin has its roots in pride. As I reflected on this truth, I began to think back on some of my wretched escapades of the past: "Now, why did I do so-and-so?" Eventually, I came to the conclusion that all of my carnal behavior could be traced to an underlying desire for self-gratification. This is pride, which is rebellion against God.

Rebellion against God is chronicled in Ezekiel 28:15-17, where we find pride to be the origin of all sin and the chief characteristic of Satan:

> You were blameless in your ways
> > from the day you were created
> > till wickedness was found in you. . . .
> So I drove you in disgrace from the mount of God,
> > and I expelled you, O guardian cherub,
> > from among the fiery stones.
> Your heart became proud
> > on account of your beauty,
> and you corrupted your wisdom
> > because of your splendor.

It is from pride that we get our self-sufficiency, which is the principal cause for the sin of prayerlessness. Therefore, God hates it, for His Word says, "God opposes the proud / but gives grace to the humble" (1 Peter 5:5).

Pride Is Competitive[6]

Pride is never satisfied with what it has, for it is constantly comparing its own vineyard with that of another brother. It measures everything in tangible units: nickels, numbers and noses; buildings, baptisms and budgets. Thus, it always wants more. In fact, it even rejoices over the misfortune of others so it can elevate self. As Lewis says, "Pride is a spiritual cancer: it eats up the very possibility of love, or contentment, or even common sense."[7]

Pride Loves Power

No one normally enters Christian service for financial remuneration, but all too frequently many become mesmerized with the power and influence. They find delight in controlling circumstances and other people; this parallels the old Navy game, "How many white hats do you have reporting to you?" I like what Plato said about power: "Those are fit to hold it who do not seek it."

Conversely, our attitude toward positions of influence should be that of humility, as outlined in Paul's epistle to the brethren at Philippi:

> Do nothing out of selfish ambition or vain conceit, but in humility consider others better than yourselves. Each of you should look not only to your own interests, but also to the interests of others.
>
> Your attitude should be the same as that of Christ Jesus:

> Who, being in very nature God,
>> did not consider equality with God
>>> something to be grasped,
> but made himself nothing,
>> taking the very nature of a servant.
>> (Philippians 2:3-7)

By the way, someone has said that humility is the only badge of Christian recognition that you don't deserve if you wear it.

Pride Robs God of His Glory

I recall Professor Howard Hendricks telling our class in seminary, "Gentlemen, there are very few men who can stand before crowds Sunday after Sunday without rendering their ministries ineffective because they have become shot through with spiritual pride!"

That platform, wherever it may be, has a tendency to seduce the most humble of people, whether they be Sunday school teachers, politicians, athletes, business leaders or pastors. No one is exempt from this deadly temptation. Therefore, we must be constantly on our faces before God, passing on all accolades to Him, for to Him alone belongs all glory. God warns us in Scripture, "I will not yield my glory to another" (Isaiah 48:11).

Pride Smothers Praise

One final thought on this issue of pride: Those who are driven by self-adulation seldom engage in effectual praise to our holy God.

This truth was driven home to my heart on the night Bill Kanaga rebuked me for my pride. As I reflected on my personal prayer life, I recognized that there was seldom any praise and worship, but just petition and intercession. Upon further reflection, the Lord disclosed that if those petitions were answered as I had requested them, then I, or those close to me, would have been the beneficiaries of most of those requests.

Through C.S. Lewis' insight and the illuminating work of the Spirit, I have learned that the more you delight in yourself and the less you delight in praising God, the worse you are becoming. And when you delight wholly in yourself and do not enter into the acknowledgment of God, you have reached the bottom—whether you realize it or not.

Throughout Scripture, pride is closely associated with wickedness. This is clearly seen in Elihu's exhortation to Job: "[God] does not answer when men cry out / because of the arrogance of the wicked. / Indeed, God does not listen to their empty plea; / the Almighty pays no attention to it" (Job 35:12-13).

If we do not learn to deal with the issue of pride swiftly and thoroughly, our prayers and intimacy with God will be greatly hindered. Victory can only be accomplished through confession with repentance and by participating in our own funerals on a daily basis. We must die to self. He must be increasing, and I must be decreasing!

Deal with It Now

I, perhaps like you, have attended many seminars and read many books with the intention to act upon the principles I learned. But to my shame, I must confess that all too frequently I have failed to put them into practice. From personal experience, I am persuaded that if you do not act upon truth within twenty-four hours after hearing it, in all probability it will become part of your library instead of your lifestyle.

My purpose in writing this book is not to add another volume to your library, but that by the grace of God you would humbly apprehend, adopt and apply these truths into your lifestyle. Has God spoken to you from the pages of this book and convicted you about certain issues? I encourage you to get alone with God in prayer about it. If you do, I am certain that the God of all comfort will bless you beyond all comprehension. We have this promise from His Word:

> But blessed is the man who trusts in the LORD,
>   whose confidence is in him.
> He will be like a tree planted by the water
>   that sends out its roots by the stream.
> It does not fear when heat comes;
>   its leaves are always green.
> It has no worries in a year of drought
>   and never fails to bear fruit.
>   (Jeremiah 17:7-8)

To help you in this process of implementation, the prayer covenant in appendix A outlines the principal issues that are central to initiating and sustaining revival in one's soul. It is not all-inclusive, so you may want to add other items that God has impressed upon your heart. The key point is to "drive a stake" in your pilgrimage of life today by which you covenant with God to make the necessary changes in order to become a more fruitful servant of our Lord Jesus Christ. As you read through this list, if God impresses you to act upon a particular item, then put a check mark in the box and move on to the next. When you are finished, sign and date it and then humbly present this to God and trust the enabling power of the Holy Spirit to help you live it. You may want to reproduce this covenant and insert it in your Bible as a daily reminder.

Study Questions

Personal Study

1. The author discusses two hindrances to prayer— loss of first love and pride—from which he says that all other sin flows. Do you agree? Are these two hindrances a problem for you?

2. Read Revelation 2:1-5. What do you think caused the church in Ephesus to lose their first love? Usually we lose our first love because we become too attached to something else. Is there anything in your life that threatens your first love?

3. In this chapter, several references are made to the eighth chapter of the book *Mere Christianity* by C.S. Lewis. Get a copy if you can and read that chapter. Do Lewis' observations match your experience?

4. Read Ezekiel 28:15-17. If pride was Satan's great sin, how do you think God reacts when He sees it in His own children?

5. The author suggests that if you have been convicted about any specific issues while reading this book, you should spend some time alone

with God in prayer. Why not take the time to do so right now?

6. Meditate on the sixth affirmation in the Prayer Covenant (see appendix A). Pray for the Lord to help you be faithful to this affirmation. Also, consider how you might implement the Scripture Praying Outline (appendix B) into your prayer life.

Group Study

1. The author begins the chapter by confessing to occasionally wandering from God. Discuss why this occurs in a Christian's life and how it can be avoided.

2. The author tells how he lost his first love because he came to love his ministry more than his Lord. Ask the members of the group if this is a problem for them. What other things in our lives can sometimes threaten to overshadow our love for God?

3. Have someone read Philippians 2:3-7. If we are to follow the example of Jesus, what are some practical ways we can concern ourselves with the interests of others and take on the attitude of a servant?

4. Scripture closely associates pride with wickedness (see, for example, Job 12-13). Why do you think this is so?

5. How does the issue of pride relate to the author's earlier concept about "participating in our own funerals on a daily basis"?

6. Close by reading together the sixth affirmation in the Prayer Covenant (see appendix A) and

praying together for the Lord to bring revival to the Church and a spiritual awakening to the world.

Appendix A: Prayer Covenant

☐ By the grace of God, and as a sanctified personal discipline, I vow to become a man/woman of prayer by learning to live in the secret closet of prayer.

> But when you pray, go into your room, close the door and pray to your Father, who is unseen. Then your Father, who sees what is done in secret, will reward you. (Matthew 6:6)

☐ I will establish a daily appointment to have quality time with my Lord in prayer.

> I rise before dawn and cry for help;
>   I have put my hope in your word.
>   (Psalm 119:147)

☐ I will learn to pray through the Scriptures.

> Establish my footsteps in Your word,
>   And do not let any iniquity have dominion
>   over me.
>   (Psalm 119:133, NASB)

☐ I will ask the Lord to search my heart for anything displeasing to Him. As I am convicted of sin, I commit myself to confess it, repent of it and by faith to be filled afresh and anew with the Holy Spirit in order to live in a continuous state of personal revival.

Search me, O God, and know my heart;
test me and know my anxious thoughts.
See if there is any offensive way in me,
and lead me in the way everlasting.
(Psalm 139:23-24)

Repent, then, and turn to God, so that your sins
may be wiped out, that times of refreshing may
come from the Lord. (Acts 3:19)

☐ I, (insert name) _____,
hereby give notice to the death of my self-life. I die to
all my:

possessions (itemize): _____
positions (itemize): _____
person (itemize): _____
privileges (itemize): _____

By signing this notice, I acknowledge that I desire to
become a servant of righteousness for the Lord Jesus
Christ. Therefore, on a daily basis, I yield my *body*,
mind, emotions, will and *spirit* to the absolute control of
God the Father, the Lord Jesus Christ and the blessed
Holy Ghost!

If anyone would come after me, he must deny himself and take up his cross daily and follow me. (Luke
9:23)

Therefore, I urge you, brothers, in view of God's
mercy, to offer your bodies as living sacrifices, holy
and pleasing to God—this is your spiritual act of
worship. Do not conform any longer to the pattern
of this world, but be transformed by the renewing of

your mind. Then you will be able to test and approve what God's will is—his good, pleasing and perfect will. (Romans 12:1-2)

☐ I will earnestly pray for the revival of my local church, the revival of the Church and for the spiritual awakening of the masses.

> Will you not revive us again,
>   that your people may rejoice in you?
>   (Psalm 85:6)

> If my people, who are called by my name, will humble themselves and pray and seek my face and turn from their wicked ways, then will I hear from heaven and will forgive their sin and will heal their land. Now my eyes will be open and my ears attentive to the prayers offered in this place. (2 Chronicles 7:14-15)

Date: _____

Signed: _____

Correspondence and conference inquiries can be addressed to:

Pray • Think • Act Ministries, Inc.
P.O. Box 267
New Wilmington, PA 16142 USA

Appendix B:
Scripture Praying Outline

The following outline is an aid to assist you in praying through selected Scriptures on a daily basis. Select the month and date to determine the Psalm or chapter of the New Testament for any given day of the year.

January/April July/October		February/May August/November		March/June September/December	
Day	Scripture	Day	Scripture	Day	Scripture
1	Psalm 1	1	Psalm 30	1	Psalm 73
2	Matthew 5:1-26	2	John 17	2	Ephesians 2
3	Psalm 3	3	Psalm 31	3	Psalm 78
4	Matthew 5:27-48	4	Acts 2:14-47	4	Ephesians 3
5	Psalm 4	5	Psalm 32	5	Psalm 80
6	Matthew 6:19-34	6	Romans 3:9-31	6	Ephesians 4
7	Psalm 5	7	Psalm 33	7	Psalm 85
8	Matthew 7	8	Romans 5	8	Ephesians 5
9	Psalm 7	9	Psalm 34	9	Psalm 91
10	Matthew 10	10	Romans 6	10	Ephesians 6
11	Psalm 10	11	Psalm 36	11	Psalm 103
12	Matthew 18:15-35	12	Romans 7	12	Colossians 1
13	Psalm 11	13	Psalm 37	13	Psalm 115
14	Mark 9:14-37	14	Romans 8	14	Colossians 2
15	Psalm 15	15	Psalm 40	15	Psalm 116
16	Mark 10:17-31	16	1 Corinthians 13	16	Colossians 3
17	Psalm 16	17	Psalm 42	17	Psalm 118
18	Luke 1:46-56, 67-80	18	Galatians 1	18	2 Timothy 2
19	Psalm 17	19	Psalm 47	19	Psalm 119:1-88
20	Luke 6:27-49	20	Galatians 2	20	2 Timothy 3
21	Psalm 18	21	Psalm 51	21	Psalm 119:89-176
22	Luke 10:1-20	22	Galatians 3	22	Hebrews 3
23	Psalm 19	23	Psalm 62	23	Psalm 126
24	Luke 11:1-13	24	Galatians 4	24	Hebrews 10
25	Psalm 23	25	Psalm 63	25	Psalm 139
26	Luke 14:15-35	26	Galatians 5	26	Hebrews 12
27	Psalm 25	27	Psalm 66	27	Psalm 145
28	John 14	28	Galatians 6	28	Hebrews 13
29	Psalm 27	29	Psalm 71	29	Psalm 146
30	John 15	30	Ephesians 1	30	Revelation 4

Notes

Introduction

1. Archibald Thomas Robertson, *Word Pictures in the New Testament, Volume 1: Matthew-Mark* (Grand Rapids, MI: Baker Book House, 1933), 51.
2. Kenneth S. Wuest, *The New Testament: An Expanded Translation* (Grand Rapids, MI: Eerdmans, 1961), 13.
3. Matthew Henry, *Matthew Henry's Commentary, Matthew to John,* vol. 5 (Grand Rapids, MI: Revell, n.d.), 71.

Chapter 1

1. Wuest, 272.

Chapter 4

1. Wuest, 13.
2. Henry, 71.
3. Wuest, 140.
4. *Sing His Praise* (Springfield, MO: Gospel Publishing House, 1991).

Chapter 6

1. Thomas A. Hand, *Augustine on Prayer* (New York: Catholic Book Publishing, 1986), 102.
2. Ibid.
3. Ibid., 103.
4. The translation I am using for the Lord's Prayer is based on the Aramaic.
5. Henry, 74.
6. Henry, vol. 3, 550.
7. Wuest, 14.

Chapter 7
1. William Temple, "The Hope of a New World," 30, quoted in Donald P. Hustad, *Jubilee! Church Music in Evangelism Tradition* (Carol Stream, IL: Hope Publishing, 1981), 78.

Chapter 8
1. James Montgomery Boice, *Psalms*, vol. 2 (Grand Rapids, MI: Baker Books, 1996), 418.
2. Sue Monk Kidd, *God's Joyful Surprise* (San Francisco: Harper Collins, 1987), 200.
3. Richard Foster, *Seeking the Kingdom* (San Francisco: Harper Collins, 1995), 62-3.
4. The twelve-page testimony of this brother is available upon request from PTAM, Inc., P.O. Box 267, New Wilmington, PA 16142.

Chapter 9
1. Dr. Charles H. Malik was the first ambassador to the United Nations from Lebanon and also one of the authors of the U.N. Charter. He had received over fifty doctorate degrees and could converse in several languages. This quotation was taken from a personal letter received by the author, dated August 23, 1983.
2. J. Edwin Orr, *Christian Commitment: Crisis and Process*, manuscript, 1984, 13; first published in London in 1951 under the title of *Full Surrender* and then edited and published in 1989 under the title of *My All His All*.
3. Ibid., 30.
4. J. Edwin Orr, "Search Me, O God." Used with permission.

Chapter 10
1. J. Edwin Orr, Lectures at the Oxford Conference for Spiritual Awakening, Oxford, England, 1982.
2. Orr, *Christian Commitment*.
3. Ibid., 15.
4. Ibid., 1-8.
5. Ibid., 19.

Chapter 11

1. C.S. Lewis, *Mere Christianity* (New York: Macmillan, 1964), 111.
2. Gerald L. Schlehr, sermon, August 13, 1995.
3. Bill Kanaga was the former CEO of the Arthur Young accounting firm.
4. Lewis, 109.
5. Ibid.
6. Ibid.
7. Ibid., 112.

Bibliography

The following is a list of books that have fostered and strengthened my communion with God.

Baqster/Lott, Anne Graham. *Daily Light*. Nashville, TN: Thomas Nelson, 1998.

Billheimer, Paul E. *Destined for the Throne*. Minneapolis: Bethany House, 1983.

Dunn, Ronald. *Don't Just Stand There, Pray Something: Secrets of Effective Prayer*. Nashville: Thomas Nelson, 1992.

Fromke, DeVern F. *The Ultimate Intention*. Cloverdale, IN: Sure Foundation, 1963.

Gordon, S.D. *Quiet Talks on Prayer*. Uhrichsville, OH: Barbour, n.d.

Grubb, Norman. *Rees Howells, Intercessor*. Fort Washington, PA: Christian Literature Crusade, 1993.

Meyer, F.B. *The Secret of Guidance*. Littleton, CO: OMF Books, 1987.

Nelson, Alan E. *Broken in the Right Place*. Nashville: Thomas Nelson, 1994.

Orr, J. Edwin. *Can God?* London: Marshall, Morgan & Scott, 1934; later edited and published under the title *Apprenticeship of Faith*, 1993.

———. *The Event of the Century*. Wheaton, IL: International Awakening Press, 1989.

———. *The Flaming Tongue*. Chicago: Moody, 1973.

———. *Full Surrender*. London: Marshall, Morgan & Scott, 1951; later revised as *Christian Commitment:*

Crisis and Process, manuscript, 1984; edited and published in 1989 under the title *My All His All.*

Sanders, J. Oswald. *Prayer Power Unlimited.* Chicago: Moody, 1977.

Spurgeon, Charles Hadden. *Morning and Evening.* Chicago: Zondervan, 1976.

Stewart, James A. *Opened Windows.* London: Marshall, Morgan & Scott, 1958.